MW01450151

THE HOLY SPIRIT AND HIS WORK

Daniel Del Vecchio

The Holy Spirit and His Work
Daniel Del Vecchio. 2019
First edition: 1970

INDEX

CHAPTER 1
Be Filled with the Spirit..................................7

CHAPTER 2
The Promise of the Father................................25

CHAPTER 3
The Coming of the Holy Spirit..........................33

CHAPTER 4
The Work of the Holy Spirit.............................45

CHAPTER 5
The Holy Spirit in the Work of Regeneration........55

CHAPTER 6
The Holy Spirit in the Work of Sanctification.......63

CHAPTER 7
The Spirit of Prayer..73

CHAPTER 8
The Gifts of the Spirit.....................................89

CHAPTER 9
Love..157

CHAPTER 10
Divine Healing..165

CHAPTER 11
Casting out Demons.......................................171

CHAPTER 1

BE FILLED WITH THE SPIRIT

The greatest need of the Church of Jesus Christ in this present time is for a powerful baptism in the Holy Spirit. Billy Graham, in a leader's meeting in California, USA, said:

> "I believe the time has come to give the Holy Spirit its proper place in our preaching, in our doctrine and in our churches. We need again to study what Saint Paul said: Be filled with the Spirit. It is needful to go over what it means to be baptized in the Holy Spirit".

The only program which will transform cities is God's program to preach the Word in demonstration of the Spirit and of power, not with the wisdom of men. The Church, the mystical body of Christ in this world, must be clean and holy, and so filled by the Spirit of God, that He will reconcile the heart and mind of the people with Himself. Nothing short of the supernatural power of the Spirit of God, will achieve this.

1. We need the Holy Spirit to receive power

In his last address to his disciples, Christ commanded them: "Not to depart from Jerusalem, but to wait for the Promise of the Father, which, He said, you have heard from Me".

Be Filled with the Spirit

"But you shall receive power when the Holy Spirit has come upon you; and you shall be witnesses to Me in Jerusalem, and in all Judea and Samaria, and to the end of the earth" (Acts 1:4,8).

They were not sent to preach, teach or set up denominations, but wait for the outpouring of the Holy Spirit and power. Therefore it is necessary to receive the baptism of the Holy Spirit in order to receive power and be a witness of Jesus Christ: in order to give proof of the Truth preached.

> "And the multitudes with one accord heeded the things spoken by Philip, hearing and seeing the miracles which he did" (Acts 8:6).

It is written of the Apostles that the Lord was working with them and confirmed the word through the accompanying signs. The baptism of the Spirit gives us the potential to be powerful witnesses, healing the sick and casting out demons. The baptism of the Spirit is not an end in itself, but a door through which we can enter and possess the gift of the Spirit and the power from on high.

Many have been deceived and discouraged, thinking that with their conversion they received the baptism of the Holy Spirit, and they do not understand why they do not have the power Christ promised. They do not enjoy the victorious overcoming life in Christ, and sometimes suffer the struggles and the weaknesses of a life without the

Spirit.

- At our conversion or regeneration, we are baptized into the body of Christ and are made partakers of the family of God. We receive the Spirit of Sonship, not the Holy Spirit.

  "And because you are sons, God has sent forth the Spirit of His Son into your hearts, crying out, Abba, Father!" (Galatians 4:6).

When we receive Christ by faith, we are made partakers of the Spirit of Christ, thus receiving the nature of God and are made new creatures. "Now if anyone does not have the Spirit of Christ, he is not His" (Romans 8:9).

"For there are three that bear witness in heaven: The Father, the Word (Christ), and the Holy Spirit; and these three are one" (1 John 5:7).

"It is evident that being born again by the power of the Holy Spirit and the Word is something altogether very different to being baptized in the Holy Spirit. A man can be regenerated by the Holy Spirit, and still not be baptized in the Holy Spirit. During the new birth, there is an impartation of Life by the power of the Spirit, and he that receives it is saved. During the baptism in the Holy Spirit, there is an impartation of power, and he who receives it is being prepared for God's service" (Dr. R. A. Torrey in his book *Presence & Work of The Holy Spirit*).

Be Filled with the Spirit

- With the baptism in the Spirit, we receive the presence of the third person of the Trinity, the Holy Spirit.

The baptism in the Spirit is not only fervor or an emotion that we feel from time to time, but it is a permanent reality that dwells inside our body, making us temples of the Holy Spirit. (1 Corinthians 3:16, 2 Corinthians 6:16).

After the revival in Samaria, through Philip's ministry, many believed and were baptized in water. These believers after having received Christ as their personal Savior were taught to seek and receive the promise of the Holy Spirit.

> "Now when the apostles who were at Jerusalem heard that Samaria had received the word of God, they sent Peter and John to them, who, when they had come down, prayed for them that they might receive the Holy Spirit. For as yet he had fallen upon none of them. They had only been baptized in the name of the Lord Jesus. Then they laid hands on them, and they received the holy spirit" (Acts 8:14-17).

We note that though they had believed and were baptized in water, they still had not received the Holy Spirit. The same event happened in Saint Paul's ministry in Ephesus. "... And finding some disciples he said to them, Did you receive the Holy Spirit when you believed?" (Observe the importance

Paul gave to the baptism in the Holy Spirit) ... So they said to him, "We have not so much as heard whether there is a Holy Spirit" (Acts 19:1-2).

These brothers in Ephesus were believers and Christ's disciples, nonetheless, just like many today, they did not know their need to receive the Holy Spirit. Saint Paul followed the same course of actions that the apostles in Samaria had followed, and with the same results. "And when Paul had laid hands on them, the Holy Spirit came upon them and they spoke with tongues and prophesied" (Acts 19:6).

- Here we see clearly that the sign of tongues follows the baptism in the Holy Spirit as in the day of Pentecost. In Cornelius' house, the same thing happened. "And those of the circumcision who believed were astonished, as many as came with Peter, because the gift of the Holy Spirit had been poured out on the Gentiles also. For they heard them speak with tongues and magnify God" (Acts 10:45-46).

Many years had gone by since the day of Pentecost and God was still giving the gift of tongues. In no place of the Holy Bible can we find any passage stating that this gift has been taken from the Church; to the contrary, Christ said that it was going to be a sign until the end of the Church's dispensation.

> "And these signs will follow those who believe: In My name they will cast out

demons; they will speak with new tongues" (Mark 16:17).

Saint Paul, upon giving the order of Service says: "Therefore, brethren, desire earnestly to prophesy, and do not forbid to speak with tongues" (1 Corinthians 14:39). The model of a Service can be found in 1 Corinthians 14:26-28.

> "How is it then, brethren? when ye come together, every one of you hath a psalm, hath a doctrine, hath a tongue, hath a revelation, hath an interpretation. Let all things be done unto edifying. If any man speaks in an unknown tongue, let it be by two, or at the most by three, and that by course; and let one interpret. But if there be no interpreter, let him keep silence in the church; and let him speak to himself, and to God".

2. The Holy Spirit is the Vicar of Christ

> "And I will pray the Father, and He will give you another Helper, that He may abide with you forever". "I will not leave you orphans; I will come to you" (John 14:16, 18).

When Christ spoke of His return to the Father, the hearts of his disciples were filled with great sorrow. The lack of Christ's presence should fill any believer's heart with sorrow. God, in His wisdom and divine love, had a great plan by which every believer may enjoy the continuous presence of the Holy Spirit.

The Lord promised: "I will come to you". Christ did not commit the work of the world's evangelization to a group of disciples neither to Peter, but to the person of the Holy Spirit. The promise of Christ's coming in the person of the Holy Spirit, encouraged the disciples and they were filled with joy. "And they worshiped Him and returned to Jerusalem with great joy" (Luke 24:52).

After the coming of the Father's promise, Christ was no more limited to the confinement of a human body, but He kept healing and working miracles through His disciples. By the power of the Spirit, the same works were carried out when the believers called on His Name. The same Spirit that dwelt in Christ had now come to dwell and abide in His believers.

> "And they went out and preached everywhere, the Lord working with them and confirming the word through the accompanying signs" (Mark 16:20).

The promise of the Holy Spirit is for you, receive Him by faith now. Jesus said: "If anyone thirsts, let him come to Me and drink" (John 7:37). Peter declared: "For the promise is to you and to your children, and to all who are afar off, as many as the Lord our God will call" (Acts 2:39).

Be Filled with the Spirit

The reason for which many believers grow cold or backslide is the lack of intimacy with God. With the gift of the Holy Spirit we can maintain a relationship of sons and friends of Christ.

The Comforter or Helper wishes to glorify Christ and draw us closer to Him. To know Christ and keep this intimate relationship, it is necessary to pray in the Spirit and to study His Word. The enemy of our souls wants to rob this intimacy to separate us from God. Many only draw close to God in public services and do not practice His presence in their daily devotionals. One of the most precious benefits that come with the Baptism in the Spirit is that of maintaining an intimate relationship with Christ.

The Holy Spirit is the Vicar of Christ on the earth and He wants to abide with us and lead us into knowing more and more of the Truth that sets free.

3. The Holy Spirit comes to glorify Christ

In the same way that Jesus came to do the works of God and to glorify the Father, the Holy Spirit has come to glorify Christ. "He will glorify Me, for He will take of what is Mine and declare it to you." (John 16:14).

The indwelling and control of the Holy Spirit in the believer also glorifies Christ. Therefore, we are responsible before God to be filled, controlled and led by the Holy Spirit. A Spirit-filled Christian will be much more useful than a hundred carnal Christians without the Spirit. The greater part God can possess of our lives, the holier and more useful we shall be for Him. The Holy Spirit does not lift the man up but glorifies Christ. When we humbly only seek the Glory of God, when all selfishness and pride are crucified, then the Holy Spirit will be able to glorify Christ through our lives.

Just as John the Baptist expressed it: "He must increase, but I must decrease." (John 3:30).

4. We need the Spirit to do the works of Christ

> "Most assuredly, I say to you, he who believes in Me, the works that I do he will do also; and greater works than these he will do, because I go to My Father" (John 14:12).

This statement of Christ has been much discussed and wrongly interpreted by the Church. This is a simple statement and must be understood exactly as it is written. The Church has done many things that never were commanded her to do, and she has overlooked the commandment of the Lord. The disciples did not try to give an obscure understanding to this promise; they simply acted with their faith, and saw the fulfillment of Christ's words. The works of Christ were evident in the ministry of men of God like Philip.

> "And the multitudes with one accord heeded the things spoken by Philip, hearing and seeing the miracles which he did. For unclean spirits, crying with a

Be Filled with the Spirit

loud voice, came out of many who were possessed; and many who were paralyzed and lame were healed" (Acts 8:6-7).

The same healing power that operated in Christ also worked in the disciples, filling them and clothing them with power from on high.

The Bible says that Philip was "full of faith and the Holy Spirit". The Holy Spirit having changed Simon (a reed) into Peter (a rock), used even his shadow to do great wonders and miracles. "So that they brought the sick out into the streets and laid them on beds and couches, that at least the shadow of Peter passing by might fall on some of them. ... and they were all healed" (Acts 5:15-16).

This great power which the apostles of old had, has not diminished, nor has it been taken away from the Church, rather it is offered to all those who are filled with the Spirit of Power. Through the gifts of the Spirit, given to the Church, we can do the works of Christ and continue His ministry on earth.

> "Verily, verily, I say unto you, He that believeth on me, the works that I do shall he do also; and greater works than these shall he do; because I go unto my Father" (John 14:12)

We have been called to do the works of God. The Lord has an individual plan for each one of His Children. These works include teaching, healing, comforting, supplying the need of the hungry, taking care of the widows and orphans.

"Pure and undefiled religion before God and the Father is this: to visit orphans and widows in their trouble, and to keep oneself unspotted from the world" (James 1:27).

5. We need the Spirit to guide and direct our lives

"However, when He, the Spirit of truth, has come, he will guide you into all truth; for He will not speak on His own authority, but whatever He hears He will speak; and He will tell you things to come" (John 16:13).

"But the Comforter, which is the Holy Ghost, whom the Father will send in my name, he shall teach you all things, and bring all things to your remembrance, whatsoever I have said unto you" (John 14:26)

The Church, the mystical body of Christ, must be directed by the Head, Christ Jesus. The Lord governs and directs through the voice and the power of the Holy Spirit.

The doctrinal errors and doctrines of demons that have entered into the Church have come through the door of carnality and wisdom of men. If we are not controlled and guided by the Spirit, we shall fail in our Christian life and shall fall into the snare of the enemy. We need to hear the voice of the Spirit in our hearts and be sensitive to His voice.

A fact without questions is that the Early Church was directed by the Holy Spirit. To illustrate this, let us mention an event in Philip's, Peter's and Paul's lives.

- "Then the Spirit said to Philip, 'Go near and overtake this chariot'" (Acts 8:29).

- "While Peter thought about the vision, the Spirit said to him, 'Behold, three men are seeking you'" (Acts 10:19).

Not only were they directed by the Spirit, but they were also prohibited by Him.

- "Now when they had gone through Phrygia and the region of Galatia, they were forbidden by the Holy Spirit to preach the word in Asia" (Acts 16:6).

We see the power of the Spirit in directing them towards a mission field and forbidding them to enter into another. Surely, the Apostles owe their great success to the direction of the Holy Spirit; He who never makes mistakes, but always leads us in paths of righteousness and usefulness for His name's sake.

When we are impulsive and impatient, we may err and not be sensitive to the voice of the Holy Spirit.

6. The Holy Spirit helps us and strengthens us in prayer

"Likewise, the Spirit also helps in our weaknesses. For we do not know what we should pray for as we ought, but the Spirit Himself makes intercession for us with groanings which cannot be uttered. Now He who searches the hearts knows what the mind of the Spirit is, because He makes intercession for the saints according to the will of God" (Romans 8:26-27).

The Spirit helps us in our weakness in that we do not know how to pray or ask as we ought to. The Holy Spirit, who knows our heart as well as the will of God, intercedes for us (the Saints) with groanings which cannot be uttered. This means that there is a prayer which is so deep, that it can only be expressed through groanings of the Spirit. The Christian who does not have the Spirit and who is not sanctified cannot understand this wonder; but if he is filled and is controlled by God, it will be to him as natural as breathing.

The same Jesus who "groaned" before Lazarus' tomb (John 11:33), who "wept" over Jerusalem and was in "agonizing" prayer in Gethsemane, is He who intercedes for us in Heaven. Before any revival or spiritual awakening, God sends the Spirit of supplication and intercession to overcome spiritual darkness and open the way.

Be Filled with the Spirit

- For the believers who have the mind of Christ, prayer is intensified by the Spirit of Prayer and Supplication.
- Without the prayer in the Spirit, we shall have little influence in the Kingdom of God and little power in our preaching and testimony.
- Without the power of the Spirit we cannot pray the prayer of faith.
- Without the power of the Spirit we will not be able to abide firm in prayer until the answer comes.
- The gift of faith is empowered by the Holy Spirit.

Besides the groanings that cannot be uttered, the Holy Spirit gives us the ability to pray in tongues for our own spiritual growth.

> "He who speaks in a tongue edifies himself" (1 Corinthians 14:4).

> "For if I pray in a tongue, my spirit prays, but my understanding is unfruitful. What is the conclusion then? I will pray with the Spirit, and I will also pray with the understanding" (1 Corinthians 14:14-15).

Of course, the Spirit guides our minds that we may pray according to the Spirit.

Nonetheless, there are times when we do not know what the mind of the Spirit is and God, who is omnificent, prays through us according to the will of God.

7. We need the Holy Spirit to worship God

Besides praying in the Spirit, worship in the Spirit is also demanded in the Word of God. The Lord himself declared:

> "God is Spirit, and those who worship Him must worship in spirit and truth" (John 4:24).

Saint Paul instructs the difference between spiritual songs and understandable songs:

> "I will sing with the spirit, and I will also sing with the understanding" (1 Corinthians 14:15)

> "Speaking to one another in psalms and hymns and spiritual songs, singing and making melody in your heart to the Lord" (Ephesians 5:19).

Again, we see the difference made between "Psalms", "Hymns" and "Spiritual songs". "Spiritual songs" are the worship songs inspired and given by the Spirit.

When we sing in the Spirit, it may include singing in unknown tongues, and our understanding abides unfruitful, but our spirit worships God.

8. The Holy Spirit imparts the gifts to the believer

The spiritual gifts are the manifestations of the Spirit who abides in the believer. Without the baptism in the Holy Spirit, we cannot have His gifts. The fruit of the Spirit begin to be manifested from our conversion, but the gifts come with the coming of the Giver, the "Holy Spirit". The fruit of the Spirit (of which a list is found in Galatians 5:22-23) is the result of a life committed to and directed by Christ. However, the gifts of the Spirit are imparted to the believers according to His will, distributing to each one as He wills.

We are exhorted to desire spiritual gifts, by this we understand that he that desires and seeks them, will also receive them.

The gifts are grouped in three categories: The gifts of revelation, the gifts of expression and the gifts of power.

Gifts of Revelation
- Word of Wisdom.
- Word of Knowledge.
- Discerning of spirits.

Gifts of Expression
- Prophecy.
- Different kinds of tongues.
- Interpretation of tongues.

We must never confuse the gift of "Different kinds of tongues" with the sign or evidence of tongues which we receive with the baptism in the Holy Spirit.

Be Filled with the Spirit

The gift of different kinds of tongues is to be used in the Church and goes together with the gift of interpretation of tongues for the edification of those who are present. (Example: First a message in tongues, and then the interpretation).

Gifts of Power.
- Gift of faith.
- Gifts of healing.
- Working of miracles.

Later on, in chapter eight, we shall study this theme of the gifts of the Spirit and we shall develop it further. For the time being sufficed to say that the gifts are given for the edification and perfecting of the Church. Without the operation of the gifts, the Church will be powerless and incomplete in several regards. The gifts must operate within the Body of Christ until the termination of the dispensation of the Holy Ghost. This will happen at the second coming of Jesus Christ.

CHAPTER 2
THE PROMISE OF THE FATHER

The Holy Spirit is eternal; just as the Father and the Son, and His works have been manifested since the creation of the world. The Holy Spirit is the fullness of the Divinity in His operating power and was and is the agent in all the creation of the universe.

He is the "finger of God" who created the expansion of the Heavens, dug up the abyss of the sea and placed the stars and the sun in their respective orbits. "In the beginning God created the heavens and the earth. ... And the Spirit of God was hovering over the face of the waters" (Genesis 1:1-2).

The Holy Spirit in the Old Testament

In the Old Testament the Holy Spirit operated in the world, speaking though the mouth of His prophets, doing miracles and wonders by the hands of His chosen servants. The Holy Spirit was not given to all, but to people chosen for a special mission. The Holy Spirit anointed Moses and the elders in the wilderness and operated the gifts in them.

> "Then the Lord ... took of the Spirit that was upon him (Moses), and placed the same upon the seventy elders; and it happened, when the Spirit rested upon

them, that they prophesied, although they never did so again" (Numbers 11:25).

"But the Spirit of the Lord came upon Gideon..." (Judges 6:34).

"And the Spirit of the Lord began to move upon him (Samson)..." (Judges 13:25).

He also came upon His servant David, the great prophet and writer of the Psalms.

The outpouring of the Holy Spirit in the New Testament

In the dispensation of the Holy Spirit which started on the day of Pentecost, His Presence is given to us as one who abides in us and dwells with us. Besides, in this dispensation, the promise of the Holy Spirit is for every believer in Christ. The prophet Joel, the great prophet of Pentecost, declared:

> "And it shall come to pass afterward That I will pour out My Spirit on all flesh; Your sons and your daughters shall prophesy, your old men shall dream dreams, your young men shall see visions. And also, on My menservants and on My maidservants, I will pour out My Spirit in those days" (Joel 2:28-29).

The words "menservants and maidservants" mean that this heavenly gift will be poured out upon the poor and humble and not only upon some chosen ones as in the days of the Old Testament. Peter

The Promise of the Father

affirmed: "for the promise is to you and to your children, and to all who are afar off, as many as the Lord our God will call" (Acts 2:39).

The Promise of the Father was foretold by the Prophet Isaiah when he said: "For with stammering lips and another tongue He will speak to this people, to whom He said, this is the rest with which You may cause the weary to rest, and, this is the refreshing" (Isaiah 28:11,12).

This prophecy is being fulfilled since the day of Pentecost, when the gift of tongues was given to the Church with the coming of the Holy Spirit. Saint Paul confirmed this when he said: "In the law it is written: With men of other tongues and other lips I will speak to this people; And yet, for all that, they will not hear me says the Lord. Therefore, tongues are for a sign, not to those who believe but to unbelievers" (1 Corinthians 14:21-22).

The disciples in obedience to Christ, waited for the Promise of the Father, just as it was commanded to them. Christ gave great importance to the coming of the Spirit when He commanded:

> "Behold, I send the Promise of My Father upon you; but tarry in the city of Jerusalem until you are endued with power from on high" (Luke 24:49).

Christ is the baptizer in the Holy Spirit. Isaiah referred to Him when he said: "Behold, a king (Christ) will reign in righteousness, ...A man will be

The Promise of the Father

as a hiding place from the wind, And a cover from the tempest, As rivers of water in a dry place, As the shadow of a great rock in a weary land" (Isaiah 32:1,2).

Christ made reference to this Scripture and to that of Isaiah 44:3 when He exclaimed in John 7:37-38:

> "On the last day, that great day of the feast, Jesus stood and cried out, saying, If anyone thirsts, let him come to Me and drink. He who believes in Me, as the Scripture has said, out of his heart will flow rivers of living water".

John the Baptist, in his preaching on the shores of the Jordan River, announced the coming of He who baptizes with the Holy Spirit. This great voice in the wilderness guided his believers to the fountain of living water.

> "I indeed baptize you with water unto repentance, but He who is coming after me is mightier than I, whose sandals I am not worthy to carry. He will baptize you with the Holy Spirit and fire" (Matthew 3:11).

Oh!! That the churches today would heed to the voice of John the Baptist and receive this baptism in the Holy Spirit and fire! It is the Holy Spirit who gives power and ability; the fire is what purifies the sons of God and capacitates them to a kingly priesthood.

The Promise of the Father

It was the fire who burned within Jeremiah's bones, setting his lips on fire with the Word of God! It was the fire burning within the apostles' hearts which gave them the impulse to spread the fire of revival to spread the Gospel everywhere.

The fire within Saint Paul, transformed cities, strengthened groups of Christians and gave them the impulse to follow Christ despite being persecuted, tormented and afflicted. The martyrs burning with the fire of the Spirit did not shrink back from at the fire which was consuming their bodies!

Oh!! That the Church in its indifference and apostasy would be newly ignited by the fire of Pentecost! All the dross and worldliness would be burnt by the Holy fire which proceeds out of the throne of God. The Church has tried to evangelize the world with its own carnal strength, raising large and luxurious buildings, etc. Presently there are more millions of souls that have never heard the Word of God, than ever before in the history of the Church. Communism, Islam, false and satanic religions are devouring multitudes, while the church sleeps in spiritual apathy!

Without the fire of the Spirit, the light of the Gospel is put out and will be overcome by the powers of darkness. Plunge your torch in the oil of the Spirit, set it on fire with prayer, and lift it up high to light this dark world!

The Holy Spirit as Comforter

In His last hours with His disciples, our Lord made a great emphasis about the coming of the Comforter. He knew that without His power we would be powerless and unable to win the multitudes for Christ.

> "And I will pray the Father, and He will give you another Helper, that He may abide with you forever; I will not leave you orphans; I will come to you" (John 14:16, 18).

Christ promised that the sadness which had inundated the hearts of his disciples, would be turned into joy by the coming of the Holy Spirit. He said:

> "Nevertheless, I tell you the truth. It is to your advantage that I go away; for if I do not go away, the Helper will not come to you; but if I depart, I will send Him to you" (John 16:7).

The Holy Spirit doing the works of Christ through us

With the going of the Lord to the Father, his redemptive work was going to be multiplied millions of times through his believers filled by the power of His Spirit. In this way Christ would not be limited by his own body, rather He would be in his believers wherever they would be.

The Promise of the Father

His same works, and greater ones, were going to be manifested with the coming of the Holy Spirit. Christ confirmed that the Holy Spirit would continue His work of convicting the world of sin, of righteousness and of judgment. He would regenerate the believer, putting God's laws in his heart and writing them in his mind.

Christ promised you:

> "Most assuredly, I say to you, he who believes in Me, the works that I do he will do also; and greater works than these he will do, because I go to My Father" (John 14:12).

The Holy Spirit has been promised by the prophets, offered by Christ our Lord, and is even now, waiting to come and dwell in you.

> "I will give you a new heart and put a new spirit within you; I will take the heart of stone out of your flesh and give you a heart of flesh. I will put My Spirit within you and cause you to walk in My statutes, and you will keep My judgments and do them" (Ezekiel 36:26-27).

CHAPTER 3

THE COMING OF THE HOLY SPIRIT

Now let us contemplate the coming of the Holy Spirit in the "Acts of the Apostles", or better said, "The Acts of the Holy Spirit".

> "When the Day of Pentecost had fully come, they were all with one accord in one place. And suddenly there came a sound from heaven, as of a rushing mighty wind, and it filled the whole house where they were sitting. Then there appeared to them divided tongues, as of fire, and one sat upon each of them. And they were all filled with the Holy Spirit and began to speak with other tongues, as the Spirit gave them utterance" (Acts 2:1-4).

The Birth of the Church

The Christian Church was conceived in an atmosphere of love, of prayer and unity. "These all continued with one accord in prayer and supplication" (Acts 1:14).

The Day of Pentecost was the Birth of the Church, when the Holy Spirit came, in fulfillment of what the Father had promised to fill and dwell in the hearts of the Master's disciples.

The Coming of the Holy Spirit

In one accord, hundred and twenty were waiting for the coming of the Comforter also promised by the Lord when He said:

> "For John truly baptized with water, but you shall be baptized with the Holy Spirit not many days from now" (Acts 1:5).

The Holy Spirit found hundred and twenty persons prepared, waiting for His Coming, and He came as a fresh wind that ran and filled the whole house. Then appeared to them divided tongues, as of fire that sat upon each one and they were all filled with the Holy Spirit and they spoke in tongues as the Spirit gave them to speak. And so, the Church was filled with the power Christ had promised. From then on, the Holy Spirit was going to be in them and not only with them. With such mighty experience and being baptized with power and love, they started to praise God with such ecstasy that it made a great sound.

> "And when this sound occurred, the multitude came together, and were confused, because everyone heard them speak in his own language" (Acts 2:6).

Besides the noise made by the hundred and twenty, the gift of tongues drew much attention, as they were hearing the wonders of God spoken in their own language. They had taken the wine of the Spirit; they had tasted the new wine and would not go back to the ceremonies and rituals of a religion based on mere formula.

The Coming of the Holy Spirit

Some of the on lookers were confused, others astonished and others mocking by saying that they were filled with wine. The outpouring of the Holy Spirit always draws attention, and many times draws censorship from the people.

If you are filled with God, you can expect that carnal men would not understand you, neither shall they appreciate the unspeakable joy you feel in your soul. Though you receive abundant criticism, you will be much more useful to the Kingdom of God than one hundred professing Christians who have not the Holy Spirit. You shall have a peace like a calmed sea and your life will be led by the Spirit in the ways of God.

Peter used this opportunity to preach Christ with new enthusiasm and a new dynamism produced in him by the infilling of the Holy Spirit. This follower of Christ was able, through the Holy Spirit, to convict three thousand souls of their sins and lead them to Christ.

> "And it shall come to pass in the last days, says God, That I will pour out of My Spirit on all flesh; Your sons and your daughters shall prophesy, your young men shall see visions, your old men shall dream dreams" (Acts 2:17)

What an amazing transformation one can observe in this humble and uneducated fisherman!

The Coming of the Holy Spirit

He who a few days earlier had denied the Lord, and was intimidated by the words of a maid, now with boldness and power accused the Jews of having killed Jesus. Then Peter testified that Christ had been resurrected from the dead and exalted to the right hand of the Father. "Therefore, being exalted to the right hand of God, and having received from the Father the promise of the Holy Spirit, He poured out this which you now see and hear" (Acts 2:33).

The Holy Spirit faithfully did His Work of convicting and reproving of sin, and then being cut to the heart, they said: "What shall we do?". Saint Peter demanded repentance and gave them the promise of the Holy Spirit. "For the promise is to you and to your children, and to all who are afar off, as many as the Lord our God will call" (Acts 2:39).

The very same Baptism the hundred and twenty received is the same Baptism for us. In God, there is no variation or shadow of turning, the same power He gave then is available for us today. If we obey the Lord and wait for this great gift in prayer and unity of the Spirit among ourselves, surely, He will come.

The Holy Spirit was poured upon the Gentiles in the house of Cornelius in the same way and with the evidence of speaking in tongues. "Can anyone forbid water, that these should not be baptized who have received the Holy Spirit just as we have?" (Acts 10:47). How did Peter know that the Gentiles had received the Holy Spirit?

The Coming of the Holy Spirit

> "And those of the circumcision who believed were astonished, as many as came with Peter, because the gift of the Holy Spirit had been poured out on the Gentiles also. For they heard them speak with tongues and magnify God" (Acts 10:45-46).

Philip descended to Samaria preached Christ to them. He had a great revival in that place; many were added to the Lord and were baptized in water.

> "But when they believed Philip as he preached the things concerning the kingdom of God and the name of Jesus Christ, both men and women were baptized" (Acts 8:12)

God had something more for Christ's disciples: that every believer should receive the seal of the Holy Spirit

The baptism of the Holy Spirit is God's way of sealing the believer.

> "In whom ye also trusted, after that ye heard the word of truth, the gospel of your salvation: in whom also after that ye believed, ye were sealed with that Holy Spirit of promise" (Ephesians 1:13).

Philip preached unto them repentance and faith, and they were baptized in water, but they knew God's work in their lives was not over; they needed the baptism of the Holy Spirit.

The Coming of the Holy Spirit

"Now when the apostles who were at Jerusalem heard that Samaria had received the word of God, they sent Peter and John to them, who, when they had come down, prayed for them that they might receive the holy spirit. For as yet He had fallen upon none of them. They had only been baptized in the name of the Lord Jesus" (Acts 8:14-16).

These in Samaria were believers in Christ, baptized in water for repentance, but the Scripture clearly says and specifies that the Holy Spirit had not come down upon them, though much time had passed since the Day of Pentecost.

By the laying on of hands

After praying for the believers, the apostles laid their hands on them for them to receive the Holy Spirit. "Then they laid hands on them, and they received the Holy Spirit" (Acts 8:17).

After the Day of Pentecost, with the exception of the occasion in Cornelius' house, many believers received the Holy Spirit by the laying on of hands. The laying on of hands is one of the fundamental doctrines of the Church.

> "Of the doctrine of baptisms, and of laying on of hands, and of resurrection of the dead, and of eternal judgment" (Hebrews 6:2).

The Coming of the Holy Spirit

Besides, the sign that indicated the receiving of the Holy Spirit was the speaking in unknown tongues. In this occasion, in Samaria, though the Holy Bible does not declare it, we do understand there was a visible manifestation since Simon –the magician– wanted to buy the gift of God which he saw was given through the Apostles' hands. "And when Simon saw that through the laying on of the apostles' hands the holy spirit was given, he offered them money". It is apparent there was an audible and visible manifestation. There is no doubt: they spoke in tongues and prophesied.

In chapter 9:17, we see Saint Paul who received the gift of the Holy Spirit by the laying on of hands. "And Ananias went his way and entered the house; and laying his hands on him he said, Brother Saul, the Lord Jesus, who appeared to you on the road as you came, has sent me that you may receive your sight and be filled with the holy spirit". In this passage of the Scripture, tongues are not mentioned as evidence, but Saint Paul in his epistle to the Corinthians said: "I thank my God I speak with tongues more than you all" (1 Corinthians 14:18).

The coming of the Holy Spirit in Ephesus is worthy of mention because it clearly shows that:
1. Tongues are the evidence or manifestation of having received the Holy Spirit;
2. That the Holy Spirit is often given by the laying on of hands;
3. That God continued baptizing in the same way as in the beginning, though by now more than

The Coming of the Holy Spirit

twenty years had gone by since the day of Pentecost.

"And when Paul had laid hands on them, the Holy Spirit came upon them, and they spoke with tongues and prophesied" (Acts 19:6).

To those who ask Him

Though we have spoken of the laying on of hands to receive the baptism, it is by no means the only way to receive the Spirit. Christ also promised Him to those who would pray with trust and faith, just as a son asks for food from his father.

"If you then, being evil, know how to give good gifts to your children, how much more will your heavenly Father give the Holy Spirit to those who ask him!" (Luke 11:13).

By the hearing of faith

Saint Paul declared to the Galatians, that they had received the Holy Spirit by the "hearing of faith", or in other words, with true faith.

"This only I want to learn from you: Did you receive the Spirit by the works of the law, or by the hearing of faith?" (Galatians 3:2).

To those who obey Him

Peter affirmed that He is given to those who obey him. "And we are His witnesses to these things,

The Coming of the Holy Spirit

and so also is the Holy Spirit whom God has given to those who obey him" (Acts 5:32).

> "There is a difference between regeneration and the Baptism with the Spirit. Those who have received Christ in their heart do not receive immediately the Holy Spirit; rather there is an interval of time. You may receive it in a moment, within an hour or within a day as in the case of Charles Finney who received it a few days later. D.L. Moody received it six months later, or in the case of Georges Bowen, it was after some years. We could also mention many more here. The period of time of waiting is not important. But what is important is that we must seek to be baptized with the Holy Spirit.

The time it takes is not important, what truly is important is that we get it and that we should know that we have it. It is true that if the apostles were not able to act as effective witnesses without this Baptism, the same is most likely to be true of us.
The Baptism in the Holy Spirit is something that only a regenerated person can receive; therefore, only a Christian can receive it. But one can be a Christian and good Christian "growing in grace and in the knowledge of the Lord Jesus Christ"; someone may be progressing in sanctification and still not have known

this Baptism. This is something that is given; it is a marvelous experience which is received once and for all; while sanctification is a continuous process".
(Excerpt of the book *Joy Unspeakable* by Martyn Lloyd Jones).

The Baptism of the Holy Spirit is for you today, it was given to the Church and so, it will abide until the end of the present dispensation, which will end with Christ's Second Coming. The self-same God who ordered, "Thou shall not kill" also commanded, "Be filled with the Spirit".

> "And these signs will follow those who believe: In My name they will cast out demons; they will speak with new tongues" (Mark 16:17).

If you have received Jesus Christ as your Savior and are obeying Him, the Holy Spirit is for you. Ask God for Him, it is God's desire and His promise for the believer.

> "He who believes in Me, as the Scripture has said, out of his heart will flow rivers of living water". But this He spoke concerning the Spirit, whom those believing in Him would receive; for the Holy Spirit was not yet given, because Jesus was not yet glorified" (John 7:38-39).

It is noteworthy to recognize that the tongues given to the 120 on the Day of Pentecost were not to

The Coming of the Holy Spirit

preach the Gospel. They spoke the "wonderful works of God". They were worshiping God, not preaching the Gospel. It was Peter's sermon that brought conviction of sin not the speaking in tongues.

> "Now when they heard this, they were pricked in their heart, and said unto Peter and to the rest of the apostles, Men and brethren, what shall we do? Then Peter said unto them, Repent, and be baptized every one of you in the name of Jesus Christ for the remission of sins, and ye shall receive the gift of the Holy Ghost" (Acts 2:37-38).

For more information, I recommend the book written by Robert Morris, *The God I Never Knew: How Real Friendship With The Holy Spirit Can Change Your Life.*

「

CHAPTER 4

THE WORK OF THE HOLY SPIRIT

We are responsible before God, the Church and the world, to be filled with the Holy Spirit. We shall also be asked to give account of all the good that we could have done, if we had been filled with the Holy Spirit. The influence of a non-spirit filled Christian in the world is very small and his example shall barely convict souls of their sins. He will lack the boldness and the power to operate the gifts. The last words of Jesus to His disciples were not to go and preach the gospel, but to wait for the promise of the Father.

The majority of members in the Evangelical Churches do not even win one soul per year for Christ. That is due to the lack of power of the Holy Spirit within them. He that lives without the Spirit shall have many friends in the world because his attitude will be similar to theirs. He will not understand much of the Bible and naturally he will lack the convicting power in his testimony. A Christian without the Spirit is very light in his living and much busy with the pleasures of the world. He will pray little and when he does his prayers will be with little faith and without power. He will have doubts concerning God's wonders, and sometimes will even be very quick to criticize the work of the Spirit being achieved in others who are being filled with the Spirit.

Instead of being wholly sanctified, these Christians without the Spirit are always asking forgiveness for their sins and they do not enjoy the perpetual peace which is in Christ.

The power of the Spirit to win souls

Christ said: "But you shall receive power when the Holy Spirit is come upon you, and you shall be my witnesses". It is not a point open to discussion that Christ plans and desires that each believer be a soul-winner. When we shall be filled with the Spirit, this is more than possible. Please note the following calculation:

If a believer would win one soul a year, and these two would win one soul each in the following year, and successively each new believer would win one soul per year, in thirty-one years two billion people would have been won for Christ. So works the law of multiplication. The Early Church grew and multiplied. It is also our model for today.

Jesus demands that each branch in Him should bear fruit. We have to take into account the quality of the fruit as well as the quantity. The Father wants us to bear much fruit, and certainly part of being fruitful is the influence that we may have in this world. If we are the Light of the World, it is necessary that we light the darkness, and this cannot be done by hiding behind the doors of our buildings. If we are the Salt of the Earth, we cannot impede the corruption of the world when we do not get out of the salt shaker.

Therefore each Christian's goal, who is born of the Spirit and filled with the Spirit, is knowing Christ better and making Him known. It is within these parameters that we should include all we do in life: to live for the Glory of God, submitted to God's revealed Will within His Word, illuminated by the Spirit and being effective witnesses of the Lord.

Without a common goal, we will not have a common destiny and we shall not be able to run the race and reach the goal to hear the Master's words, saying: "'Well done, good and faithful servant; you were faithful over a few things, I will make you ruler over many things".

When we are filled with the Holy Spirit

Many times, a Spirit-filled Christian will be called an eccentric by carnal Christians; and rightfully so, because the latter do not understand the motives, nor the impulses of the Spirit of God. The carnal mind will always be enmity against God and does not understand the things of the Spirit, because these must be spiritually discerned.

> "Because the carnal mind is enmity against God: for it is not subject to the law of God, neither indeed can be" (Romans 8:7).

A Spirit-filled Christian will feel great responsibility for the Church and the unbelievers. The Holy Spirit is concerned with the Kingdom of God and the conversion of the world.

The Work of the Holy Spirit

"For those who live according to the flesh set their minds on the things of the flesh, but those who live according to the Spirit, the things of the Spirit" (Romans 8:5).

Those filled with the Spirit will spend much time in prayer for the lost souls and will feel much sadness for the condition of apathy in the Church. When we are filled with the Holy Spirit, holiness and separation from the world will be manifested in our lives.

The indwelling of the Holy Spirit will separate the believer from the world, from the fleshly hobbies and the non-beneficial activities of life. Your worldly friends will forsake you because they will not understand your actions or your new ideas. You will be led by a different Spirit and therefore will have impulses for a different direction. If you are filled with the Spirit, you will have peace with God and with your conscience. You will not continuously be tormented with insecurity about your salvation, or heavy-laden by a conscience in turmoil. Though temptations will be greater each time, the Spirit of God will defend you at all times.

If you are filled with the Holy Spirit you can expect much opposition from the carnal Christians within the Church; since they will always oppose any idea leading to the putting off of their indifference. The devil is not in the least concerned by carnal Christians because these do not oppose him, neither do they attack him.

The Work of the Holy Spirit

When we shall be filled with the Holy Spirit, then, we will be a threat to Satan and we can expect persecution even from those who profess Christianity. Holiness has never been very popular in the world and the majority usually rejects the light that reveals their sin and hypocrisy.

If you are filled with the Spirit, you will have peace in tribulation, and quietness in affliction. Though these trials will sometimes be difficult, you shall have the help of the Spirit and peace in your soul.

The Holy Spirit will see to it that the fruit of the Spirit will grow in your life. With our conversion we start seeing the manifestation of the fruit of the Spirit, but with the baptism in the Spirit, the fruit will noticeably mature in every way. God's desire is that we bear fruit and fruit in abundance and perfection.

> "But the fruit of the Spirit is love, joy, peace, longsuffering, kindness, goodness, faithfulness, gentleness, self-control. Against such there is no law" (Galatians 5:22-23).

> "I am the vine, you are the branches. He who abides in Me, and I in him, bears much fruit; for without Me you can do nothing" (John 15:5).

The different characteristics of this fruit are produced by the Spirit and not by the carnal efforts.

The Work of the Holy Spirit

These are perfected in our lives when we humbly surrender to God's will. Seek to be filled with the Holy Spirit and live in such a way as is pleasing to God. In this way His influence will manifest with greater intensity in your life. The will of God is that we be temples of the Holy Spirit, built up as living stones, to be a habitation of God in the Spirit. "And do not be drunk with wine, in which is dissipation; but be filled with the Spirit" (Ephesians 5:18). Amen.

The baptism of the Holy Spirit will not resolve all of your problems, but it will introduce a fountain of life into your Christian experience, making possible a more effective and fruitful service.

What are the prerequisites for the reception of the Holy Spirit? We must understand that we will never, of ourselves, come to the place of sufficient goodness or holiness, whereby we might hope to merit any gift of God. All God's gifts are given by grace and received by faith. "... and that not of yourselves; it is the gift of God, not of works, lest anyone should boast" (Ephesians 2:8-9). A person filled with the Spirit is not "better" than another who has not as yet received this baptism, although he is in a position infinitely better to grow. I do not want to say that he is more holy, but simply that he has accepted by faith a gift that God has made available to all of his children.

Dr. W. E. Sangster writes:
"When we have the Spirit, we have all that we can ever desire to have. The Holy Spirit is the greatest

gift God can give us. When he gives us the Spirit, he gives us every precious thing with Him. When he gives us the Spirit, he gives us himself. Jesus promised the Spirit to his disciples. He said: If you love me, keep my commandments. And I will pray the Father, and he shall give you another Comforter, that he may abide with you forever; Even the Spirit of truth, whom the world cannot receive, because it seeth him not, neither knoweth him: but ye know him; for he dwelleth with you and shall be in you" (John 14:15-17).

> "If a man loves me, he will keep my words; and my Father will love him, and we will come unto him, and make our abode with him" (John 14:23).

The promise of the Spirit is for those who love him. It is for those who thirst for him. It is for those who desire to obey him as Lord. It is for those who ask; with the faith of a child. Children may ask their father for bread, or for meat, or for an egg. Jesus said: "If you then, being evil, know how to give good gifts unto your children, how much more shall your heavenly Father give the Holy Spirit to them that ask: him?" (Luke 11:13).

If you believe as a rule that you were baptized with the Spirit on the day that you were converted, it is improbable that you will ask: in faith.

If you are not thirsty and desirous above all things to be filled, you probably will not receive this baptism. Andrew Murray writes:

The Work of the Holy Spirit

"Whenever a Christian begins to strive for the attainment of this blessing, he generally puts forth a series of efforts in order to reach faith, obedience, humility, and submission which are conditions for obtaining the blessing. When he does not receive the hoped for blessing, he is tempted to blame himself; and if he still has any energy left he continues on in the same way with even greater effort and more zeal. This great battle is not in vain, nor is it entirely useless. It has its purpose, although not in the way that had been foreseen. It accomplishes the same function as the law, that is to say, it teaches us our total impotence. It leads us to that desperate situation in which we are finally disposed to give God the place that he must have. Actually, this lesson is indispensable.

I cannot grant this blessing to myself, nor can I take it. It is only God who can work it in me." (Excerpt from the book: *Piedras Fundamentales*, also by Daniel Del Vecchio).

CHAPTER 5
THE HOLY SPIRIT IN THE WORK OF REGENERATION

> "And when He has come, He will convict the world of sin, and of righteousness, and of judgment: of sin, because they do not believe in Me" (John 16:8-9).

The Holy Spirit works in conjunction with the Word of God in the conversion of souls. From the beginning to the end, He is the agent that operates in the regeneration of the believer. The Holy Spirit is He who wields the sword of the Word of God.

> "For the word of God is living and powerful, and sharper than any two-edged sword, piercing even to the division of soul and spirit, and of joints and marrow, and is a discerner of the thoughts and intents of the heart" (Hebrews 4:12).

> "And take the helmet of salvation, and the sword of the Spirit, which is the word of God" (Ephesians 6:17).

The four stages the unbeliever goes through

The Holy Spirit awakens the sinner by using the Word and warns him of his danger.

The Holy Spirit in the Work of Regeneration

He convicts of the sin of unbelief until the unbeliever, being *awakened*, is convicted of his guilt. The sin of unbelief is the sin that leads to eternal loss and is the sin that conceives the other sins. Christ said that the Holy Spirit would convict the world of sin, "because they do not believe in Me" (John 16:9).

In the first place the sinner is *indifferent* to his rebellion against God and lives apparently forgetful of his own danger. When the Word of God is preached, by directing it to his personal situation, the Spirit of God stirs the sinner's conscience until the sense of the fear of God and remorse for his sin are awakened.

Then the sinner, being awakened, enters in the third stage of his conversion and is *convicted*. In this condition he trembles at the cliff of hell and at this stage his soul fights in the valley of indecisiveness until he submits to God. The Holy Spirit goes after him with the Word, uncovering his heart, and reminding him of his rebellion. In this condition the Spirit also reveals Christ as his substitute (The sacrifice for his sins).

When the sinner, believing in Christ as his only Savior, *submits* to the will of God, the Spirit operates the work of renewing and regenerating his heart and spirit. He is made a new creature in Christ, regenerated and justified by his faith. Flesh can change flesh, the mind can educate and renew the mind, but only the Spirit of God can transform the spirit of men. "Jesus answered, "Most

The Holy Spirit in the Work of Regeneration

assuredly, I say to you, unless one is born of water and the Spirit, he cannot enter the kingdom of God" (John 3:5).

The Holy Spirit sows the seed of the Word of God in the open heart and feeds it until the nature of Christ is conceived in the heart.

> "Having been born again, not of corruptible seed but incorruptible, through the word of God which lives and abides forever" (1 Peter 1:23).

You can be used by God to win lost souls. It is a work that requires great wisdom and knowledge. For example: The surgeon can take a life by a simple error of his hand; likewise, with an ill expressed word, you can give false comfort to a person who can lose his conviction of sin. Every testimony or preaching must lead the souls to the expiatory sacrifice of Christ.

The simple Gospel is "the power of God to those who are being saved". (See 1 Corinthians 1:18). By the Scriptures you must *awaken* the indifferent sinner, showing him the danger of his position without Christ.
The Word must be used as a sword which penetrates into the inner parts of the heart revealing to the sinner his unbelief and transgression.

"The heart is deceitful above all things, And desperately wicked; Who can know it?" (Jeremiah 17:9).

The minister or the personal worker needs to discern on what point the Spirit is speaking to the sinner and continue on this point until he submits to God

The sinner always seeks excuses and places to hide. "... For we have made lies our refuge, and under falsehood we have hidden ourselves" (Isaiah 28:15). At the present time, there are millions hiding under the cloak of religion and good works, etc. But God will dismiss every lie with his Word. When Adam sinned, he tried to hide amongst the trees of the Garden. The voice of God penetrating into his souls, said: "Where are you?" (See Genesis 3:9).

The Spirit of God uncovers the hypocrisy of the heart until repentance is the outcome. When the sinner is well *convicted* and cut to the heart until he shouts: "What shall I do?" then you can show him the Lamb of God which takes away the sin of the world. It is impossible to bring the sinner to Christ, without him acknowledging his need to be saved and redeemed. If you are led by the Spirit, He will give you the necessary wisdom for souls to accept the Light of the Gospel.

The sinner will prefer doing anything but surrendering with a sincere heart to God and accept His mercy.

The Holy Spirit in the Work of Regeneration

With this in mind, do not give him any place of rest, unless it is in Christ. No good works can ever save us and only on the Rock will we be safe. We are justified by the faith of Christ, and not by the works of the law, "... for by the works of the law no flesh shall be justified" (Galatians 2:16).

Never try to convince the sinner that he is saved, but wait for the Spirit to give witness to his spirit that he is a son of God.

> "The Spirit Himself bears witness with our spirit that we are children of God" (Romans 8:16).

> "To redeem those who were under the law, that we might receive the adoption as sons" (Galatians 4:5).

He will need to have personal confidence and will obtain it, if in submitting to God, he places all his faith in Christ. The Holy Spirit will glorify Christ and will reveal the vicarious sacrifice of the cross which shall justify all who believe. "Therefore, having been justified by faith, we have peace with God through our Lord Jesus Christ" (Romans 5:1). Saint Paul counseled the jailer in the city of Philippi: "Believe on the Lord Jesus Christ, and you will be saved". (Acts 16:31) But what does it mean to believe in Jesus Christ? There are many who believe they are saved and think that this is the saving faith.

The Holy Spirit in the Work of Regeneration

One may believe that he is saved, in any religion, and be completely lost. Others think that having received the Lord Jesus Christ, they are now secure. But Christ puts conditions to be his disciples. He said that whoever does not forsake all that he has cannot be his disciple. There is a price to pay.

> "Because strait is the gate, and narrow is the way, which leadeth unto life, and few there be that find it" (Matthew 7:14).

To believe in the Lord Jesus, is to trust that He is the Son of God who was crucified, paying our debt for our sins: It is to believe that He redeemed us from death and from sin; It is to trust in His Sacrifice, His death and Resurrection, His finished and forever perfected work, and that He is now seated at the right-hand of God the Father. It is to believe that the blood of Christ cleanses us of all sins, and that by faith we are justified and have peace with God.

> "For God so loved the world that He gave His only begotten Son, that whoever believes in Him should not perish but have everlasting life. For God did not send His Son into the world to condemn the world, but that the world through Him might be saved. He who believes in Him is not condemned; but he who does not believe is condemned already, because he has not believed in the name of the only begotten Son of God" (John 3:16-18).

The Holy Spirit in the Work of Regeneration

Saint Peter, in his first preaching, on the day of Pentecost, clarified very well the way to be saved, stating that it is necessary to repent. He said: "Repent and let every one of you be baptized in the name of Jesus Christ for the remission of sins; and you shall receive the gift of the Holy Spirit" (Acts 2:38). It is clear that no one will repent without acknowledging that he is mistaken. Peter accused them to be accomplices in the death of Christ, for this reason they were cut to the heart and asked, "Men and brethren, what shall we do?". The sinner, while in his state of indifference and spiritual sleep, does not seek a remedy, until he is convinced that he is lost and in danger of hell. It is the word of God, made effective by the Holy Spirit that produces the New Birth.

My desire it that God would use you to win souls. That your tongue, being guided by the Holy Spirit, you would sow the incorruptible seed of the Word of God. "Those who sow in tears shall reap in joy" (Psalm 126:5).

CHAPTER 6
THE HOLY SPIRIT IN THE WORK OF SANCTIFICATION

In this chapter, of the work of sanctification in the believer, we will not be able to cover the whole theme in all its various aspects; we only want to show you this great blessing as something we must desire. Sanctification operates progressively in the life of the Christian. The Lord who commanded "Be filled with the Spirit", also ordered "Be holy, for I am holy" (1 Peter 1:16). If we are children of the Holy God, naturally Holiness that characterizes Him must have its fruit in us, His children. "Therefore be imitators of God as dear children" (Ephesians 5:1).

Included within the work of sanctification, we have the works of separation, purification, and consecration.

- In the Regeneration, God operates the separation from the World, and from an unclean life filled with vices.
- In the experience of the new Birth, we are new creatures in Christ Jesus, propelled and led by a new spirit. "Regeneration" and the "New Birth" are two words describing the same event.
- In Sanctification, the Spirit not only continues the work of separation, but He adds consecration to God and His work.

The Holy Spirit in the Work of Sanctification

We are not merely separated from sin but are consecrated to God. With sanctification, the work is more absolute and permanent; consecration to God and His purposes is essential in the believer. The Holy Spirit takes hold of the sword of the Word to clean our lives and prepare the branch to bear much fruit. Christ said to his disciples: "You are already clean because of the word which I have spoken to you" (John 15:3). God's purpose in sanctifying the believer is that he may bear "much fruit" and "more fruit".

> "Every branch in Me that does not bear fruit He takes away; and every branch that bears fruit He prunes, that it may bear more fruit" (John 15.2).

The Life of Christ within us bears the fruit of the Spirit, but sanctification guarantees the vinedresser (God) that these fruits are produced in abundance and in perfection.

The Spirit often employs means that are grueling for us, until He can appreciate the desired results in our lives. Even in our afflictions due to the trials, if we know that God is operating for our sanctification, we can join with Saint Paul when he said:

> "And we know that all things work together for good to those who love God, to those who are the called according to His purpose" (Romans 8:28).

Proof of sanctification is humility before God and men

Humility is the fruit and perfection of holiness. Someone has said that the essence of sin is selfishness. Satan operates through self. There is no selfishness more hidden and more dangerous than the pride of our holiness. Pride is one of the greatest obstacles in way of holiness, and is an abomination to God. "Keep to yourself, do not come near me, For I am holier than you! These are smoke in My nostrils, A fire that burns all the day" (Isaiah 65:5).

In each one of us the Pharisee and the Publican can be found, and both come together to worship God. We can know the Pharisee when he comes openly and lifts himself up, but what is dangerous is when he clothes like the Publican, apparently humble, although inwardly he is still a Pharisee. He that seeks holiness must walk in the way of humility and in all occasions, he must humble himself under the hand of God. "Therefore humble yourselves under the mighty hand of God, that He may exalt you in due time" (1 Peter 5:6). This is God's command and what we must do; and when the occasion comes, He will exalt us in His time.

Humility is death to our own desires and God's ascension on the throne of our heart

Someone well said that humility is not thinking less of yourself, but rather thinking of yourself less.

The Holy Spirit in the Work of Sanctification

When God is the all in all for us, and "to live is Christ", self has no place, because it has been crucified. (See Galatians 2:20).

We must be submitted to God in all our thinking and decisions; submitted in our wills and desires. When our will is lost in the river of God's will, it produces in us the true humility which is the perfection of holiness.

When a river flows into the sea it loses its own identity, but gains a thousand times more power as it is united as part of the sea. In the same way, we ourselves, when we submit the "I", we are united in humility with Christ, and become a channel of blessings that God will use for life and salvation to the multitudes.

We must desire holiness in such a way, that we would glory in anything or any experience that humbles us.

> "And He said to me, My grace is sufficient for you, for My strength is made perfect in weakness. Therefore most gladly I will rather boast in my infirmities, that the power of Christ may rest upon me. Therefore I take pleasure in infirmities, in reproaches, in needs, in persecutions, in distresses, for Christ's sake. For when I am weak, then I am strong" (2 Corinthians 12:9-10).

Humility gives way to the power and glory of Christ upon us

Saint Paul acknowledged that humility gives way to power and to holiness, and it is where the power and the glory of Christ dwells upon us. Only the revelation of the cross and the Grace of God, will humble us at the feet of the humble Jesus of Nazareth. Humility is the beauty of Christ and the atmosphere of heaven. It was selfishness and pride, that caused Lucifer's fall from being "the anointed cherub who covers" to becoming the vilest serpent.

> "For you have said in your heart: 'I will ascend into heaven, I will exalt my throne above the stars of God; I will also sit ...I will ascend above the heights of the clouds, I will be like the Most High" (Isaiah 14:13-14).

> ... "Thus says the Lord God: "You were the seal of perfection, Full of wisdom and perfect in beauty. You were in Eden, the garden of God...".

> ... "You were the anointed cherub who covers; I established you; You were on the holy mountain of God...".

> ... "You were perfect in your ways from the day you were created, till iniquity was found in you...

> ... "You became filled with violence within, and you sinned; Therefore I cast you as a

profane thing Out of the mountain of God; And I destroyed you, O covering cherub...".

... "Your heart was lifted up because of your beauty; You corrupted your wisdom for the sake of your splendor..." (Ezekiel 28:12-17).

"Because you have done this, you are cursed" (Genesis 3:14).

It was pride that sank the human race into the misery of sin and its terrible consequences. It was pride also that worked in Eve when Satan promised her: "... you will be like God, knowing good and evil" (Genesis 3:5).

As pride brought us all the evil that exists, so spiritual humility brings us sanctification and freedom from the curse

Christ revealed to us the power of humility when he came in the likeness of flesh, as a man, born in the manger and dying the most ignominious form of death that existed "the death of the cross". "But (Christ) made Himself of no reputation, taking the form of a bondservant, and coming in the likeness of men. And being found in appearance as a man, He humbled Himself and became obedient to the point of death, even the death of the cross" (Philippians 2:7,8).

Christ surrendered to the will of God and leaving His supreme position in Heaven, he came to place

The Holy Spirit in the Work of Sanctification

us with Him in heavenly places. "And raised us up together and made us sit together in the heavenly places in Christ Jesus" (Ephesians 2:6).

If you want to rescue and raise fallen people humble yourself under the hand of God. If you want to be perfect in holiness, clothe yourself with the humble mind of Christ.

> "Let this mind be in you which was also in Christ Jesus, who, being in the form of God, did not consider it robbery to be equal with God, but made himself of no reputation, taking the form of a bondservant, and coming in the likeness of men" (Philippians 2:5-7).

With the death of our carnal desires, humility is perfected and with the perfection of humility, sanctification is complete. The highest degree of holiness is found in true humility. Do not seek to be powerful in the things of God; desire holiness and the power of God will be upon your life.

By faith we appropriate the work Christ finished and perfected

In this work the Holy Spirit is the agent at work; the flesh cannot overcome the flesh. Satan cannot cast out Satan. Thank God the work is already finished and perfected forever.

Christ's Death gives us power over sin and the old man. Christ's Ascension gave us the power of the Holy Spirit that we may appropriate for ourselves

The Holy Spirit in the Work of Sanctification

the victory over the 'I'. Though Christ died for the sins of the whole world, we are not saved until by faith, we appropriate for ourselves the redemption of Christ.

By faith, the blood of Christ cleanses us from all sin.

By faith, we are justified and have peace with God. This is not merely in our thinking, rather faith works the change in our lives, and we are born again.

Faith moves the Holy Spirit and He in turn operates the transformation in us. In the same way, sanctification operates in us when we make ours the Death of Christ. Faith progressively operates in us sanctification and purification of the spirit. Sanctification comes by making Christ's Holiness ours.

It is the Life of Christ operating in us that works the death to self and of the carnal desires of the old man. Saint Paul experienced this death and reveals it in his epistle. "I have been crucified with Christ; it is no longer I who live, but Christ lives in me; and the life which I now live in the flesh I live by faith in the Son of God, who loved me and gave Himself for me" (Galatians 2:20).

We have a new law that operates in us, the law of eternal life, the law of the Holy Spirit, which makes us free from the law of sin and death.

The Holy Spirit in the Work of Sanctification

"For the law of the Spirit of life in Christ Jesus has made you free from the law of sin and death" (Romans 8:2). Sin operates in us eternal death, but holiness is the power of eternal life operating in us. Sanctification is a progressive work achieved by the Spirit of Life, until the "seed" of Christ in us, achieves its complete work.

"But put on the Lord Jesus Christ, and do not think of providing for the lusts of the flesh" (Romans 13:14). Do not pay attention to Satan's voice, rather be affirmed in what God says to us. God has made Christ to be for us our wisdom and our sanctification.

> "But of Him you are in Christ Jesus, who became for us wisdom from God; and righteousness and sanctification and redemption; that, as it is written, "He who glories, let him glory in the Lord" (1 Corinthians 1:30-31).

Let us submerse ourselves in the greatness of the revelation of our union with Christ. We are identified with him in his death, in his resurrection and in his Eternal Life in the heavenly places. "For in Him dwells all the fullness of the Godhead bodily; and you are complete in him, who is the head of all principality and power" (Colossians 2:9-10).

The authority of Christ with the believer exceeds our comprehension but we know that as He is, so are we in this world.

The Holy Spirit in the Work of Sanctification

"For both He who sanctifies and those who are being sanctified are all of one father, for which reason He is not ashamed to call them brethren" (Hebrews 2:11). We are one with Him, who sanctifies us if we hold our faith firm until the end. We are one with Him in His Death, one with Him in His Resurrection, and one with Him in His Exaltation. "He is our hope of Glory" (see Colossians 1:27).

AMEN.

CHAPTER 7

THE SPIRIT OF PRAYER

"Likewise the Spirit also helps in our weaknesses. For we do not know what we should pray for as we ought, but the Spirit Himself makes intercession for us with groanings which cannot be uttered. Now He who searches the hearts knows what the mind of the Spirit is, because He makes intercession for the saints according to the will of God" (Romans 8:26-27).

Born of the Spirit or born of the flesh?

The coldness and apathy which prevails in the Church nowadays, is proof of the lack of the Spirit of Prayer. On a general basis, the Church is begetting sons "born of the flesh" who know nothing of the Spirit of Prayer, which was predominant in the early Church. Without this spirit we cannot expect spiritual fruits in the Church neither hope to be used in the Kingdom of God. Just as in the natural, without pain there is no giving birth, in the same way, without the Spirit of Prayer there will be no spiritual children. With the indifference which is so prevalent in the Church, it is very difficult, if not impossible, that sinners be cut to the heart and converted.

The Spirit of Prayer

If it is the Holy Spirit who transforms the sinner into a "new Creature in Christ", then without His power it is clear that souls will not be born again.

Saint Paul knew well the Spirit of Prayer and His power to convict and bring souls to the feet of Christ. He told the carnal Church of the Galatians: "My little children, for whom I labor in birth again until Christ is formed in you" (Galatians 4:19). It was the ministry of prayer, day and night, that gave him so many spiritual sons. Of a truth he was able to say:

> "For though you might have ten thousand instructors in Christ, yet you do not have many fathers; for in Christ Jesus I have begotten you through the gospel" (1 Corinthians 4:15).

What is born of the flesh, is flesh; and what is born of the Spirit is spirit

The Church of Christ is called to be the mother of spiritual sons, sons of God, conceived in an atmosphere of love and prayer. For the lack of the Spirit of Prayer in the Church, some become "believers" but without power or influence for Christ. These are sons born of the flesh and converted with the mind, but still having the works of the flesh manifested in them. One can be a good church member; he may also partake of the sacraments; may be an excellent helper and be present at every meeting. Nonetheless, if he does everything with the idea of meriting his salvation, it is useless.

The Spirit of Prayer

"He who has the Son has life; he who does not have the Son of God does not have life" (1 John 5:12).

As the mother is, so are her children; If the church does not come to experience the Spirit of Prayer and supplication, she will beget a generation of "Christians" but without the nature of Christ.

> "For it is written that Abraham had two sons: the one by a bondwoman, the other by a freewoman. But he who was of the bondwoman was born according to the flesh, and he of the freewoman through promise, which things are symbolic. For these are the two covenants: the one from Mount Sinai which gives birth to bondage, which is Hagar; for this Hagar is Mount Sinai in Arabia, and corresponds to Jerusalem which now is, and is in bondage with her children; but the Jerusalem above is free, which is the mother of us all. For it is written: Rejoice, O barren, you who do not bear! Break forth and shout, you who are not in labor! For the desolate has many more children Than she who has a husband. Now we, brethren, as Isaac was, are children of promise. But, as he who was born according to the flesh then persecuted him who was born according to the Spirit, even so it is now" (Galatians 4:22-29).

Would this not be the cause for which we have so many divisions and contentions? The sons of the flesh will always oppose the things of the Spirit and set themselves against both the mind of God and His sons.

It is the Spirit that gives life, reproves and convicts of sin

It is in the secret room of prayer that the power of God to convict and change heart is produced. It is by the power of the Spirit that the Word purifies and gives the new birth into the family of God. It is by the Life of the Spirit that the preacher may be used of God to bring conviction of sin and of the coming judgment, until the soul trembles in agony of conviction of sin until he submits to God. God does not have grand-children, only sons begotten by His Word and by His Spirit.

> "Who were born, not of blood, nor of the will of the flesh, nor of the will of man, but of god" (John 1:13).

The three thousand converted on the Day of Pentecost were cut to the heart, and called out in agony of spirit:

> "Men and brethren, what shall we do?" They were born again in the atmosphere of the Spirit of Prayer of the upper room. It was the midnight prayer of Paul and Silas in the prison, which broke the jailer's heart until he cried out: "Sirs, what must I do to be saved?" (Acts 16:30).

The Spirit of Prayer

The church has lost much of the Spirit of Prayer; to such a level that iniquity feels very much at ease next to holiness. Instead of this, we must repent and seek the Spirit until sin must be confessed and cleansed.

1. There are no powerful Christians in Christ without being filled with the Spirit of Prayer.

2. There is no message or sermon that will reprove the unconverted, without being conceived in the Spirit of Prayer.

3. Without the Spirit of Prayer, our supplications will be weak and will lack power and faith.

4. Without the Spirit of Prayer, there won't be much interest for the souls lost without Christ.

5. It is the Holy Spirit who helps us in our weakness, until he gives us the groanings in the spirit according to the will of God.

6. When the Spirit guides us in prayer for something, we can have the assurance that God wants to grant the answer.

7. It is by the Spirit that we can pray the prayer of faith. "And the prayer of faith will save the sick, and the Lord will raise him up. And if he has committed sins, he will be forgiven." (James 5:15).

The Spirit of Prayer

8. It is the Spirit of Prayer that empowers us to abide hours in agony of spirit, until God moves every obstacle.

9. The Spirit fills our minds with the state of the Church and of the world, until we feel deeply the need to pray for them.

The prayer of the Spirit is sometimes so deep, that it cannot be expressed but with "groanings that cannot be uttered" and with weeping. It was the influence of the Spirit in the Garden of Gethsemane, which prepared the Lord for the test of Calvary, when he "offered up prayers and supplications, with vehement cries and tears..., and was heard" (Hebrews 5:7). If we have much of the Spirit of Christ in us, He will manifest Himself in us as the Spirit of Prayer and supplication.

Many think that being filled of the Spirit; they will always be completely joyful. If we look at Christ and the Prophets, we will see that this is not so; the prophets of old, filled with the Spirit were crying and groaning because of the sin of the people of God. Listen to Jeremiah when he says: "O my soul, my soul! I am pained in my very heart! My heart makes a noise in me; I cannot hold my peace, Because you have heard, O my soul, The sound of the trumpet, The alarm of war" (Jeremiah 4:19). Only those who have not the Spirit may abide indifferent and lethargic in the face of the state of the world and of the Church.

The Spirit of Prayer

Let us now cite some of the causes which prevent us from having the Spirit of Prayer.

1. For the lack of practice in praying

It is very rare to find, nowadays, a Christian who prays sufficiently. Even amongst ministers and workers, the lack of prayer is considerable. The "Marthas" are more prevalent than the "Marys". God has many servants who are always working for him, but how few are at His feet and have learned to work with him. Mary pleased the Lord more than Martha because she found the secret of the Fellowship with the Lord. The little we do being filled with the Spirit of Prayer will avail much more than what we do in our own strength. Many of our efforts are in vain, because we have not first waited in prayer. With these truths in mind, let us decide that from now on we will dedicate more time to prayer. When we are regularly in the presence of God, it is much easier to have much of the Spirit of Prayer.

We must not confound praying, with the Spirit of Prayer, because it is not the same. We can pray with the understanding without the help of the Spirit of Prayer. "What is it then? I will pray with the spirit, and I will pray with the understanding also" (1 Corinthians 14:15). We have the commandment to pray "praying always with all prayer and supplication in the Spirit, being watchful to this end with all perseverance and supplication for all the saints" (Ephesians 6:18).

The Spirit of Prayer

It is the Grace of God that grants His Spirit to help us and guide us in prayer, but it is our duty to pray; for He has promised to send us His Spirit, who makes intercession for us and in us.

The prayer in the Spirit is given to us firstly because "we know not what we should pray". Secondly, His influence increases our faith to obtain the answer. If you want to get the Spirit of Prayer, pray much, until your mind and attitude be such, that God may grant His Spirit. If you are baptized with the Holy Spirit, and if daily you have your time of prayer, you can expect His power in you.

Besides the "groanings that cannot be uttered" the Spirit prays through us in other tongues. "For if I pray in a tongue, my spirit prays, but my understanding is unfruitful. For he who speaks in a tongue does not speak to men but to god, for no one understands him; however, in the spirit he speaks mysteries. He who speaks in a tongue edifies himself" (1 Corinthians 14:14,2,4).

We must note that the Scriptures demand that we pray with the understanding that we pray in tongues and pray in the Spirit.

> "Praying always with all prayer and supplication in the Spirit, being watchful to this end with all perseverance and supplication for all the saints" (Ephesians 6:18).

2. For the lack of care and love

Let's have a look at a mother whose child is very sick. She is agitated and groaning with the burden. At all times her child is on her mind, she does not think at anything else but his physical condition. Why? Because she loves him, and cares for him. Without the love of God for souls and for God's interests, we cannot have the Spirit of Prayer. God is love and those filled with God, will have love tor their neighbor. If you have the love of God, you will not be able to live foreign to the needs of this world nor of the church.

> "If someone says, "I love God," and hates his brother, he is a liar; for he who does not love his brother whom he has seen, how can he love God whom he has not seen?" (1 John 4:20).

The Love of God will bring us the Spirit of Prayer, which characterizes the children of God; who love in such a way that they give themselves in prayer for the world. "Jesus said to Simon Peter, Simon, son of Jonah, do you love Me more than these? He said to Him, Yes, Lord; You know that I love You. He said to him, Feed My lambs" (John 21:15).

3. For the lack of discipline in our lives

The spirit of Christ is occupied with the things of the Father. The spirit of frivolity or levity which characterizes the world, does not have part with the children of God.

We must live truly believing in the reality of hell and that God's judgment will come upon the children of disobedience. It is due to this lack of seriousness and gravity of some Christians that many are not converted, when they see that by our lives and actions, we apparently do not believe what is preached.

> "Teaching us that, denying ungodliness and worldly lusts, we should live soberly, righteously, and godly in the present age" (Titus 2:12).

> "Neither filthiness, nor foolish talking, nor coarse jesting, which are not fitting, but rather giving of thanks" (Ephesians 5:4).

If you get a chance to listen to many Christians in their conversations for just five minutes, you will be able to understand why they do not have much of the Spirit of Prayer. "In the multitude of words sin is not lacking, But he who restrains his lips is wise" (Proverbs 10:19). I have never seen a talkative Christian with much of the Spirit of Prayer. Let us learn to refrain our tongue. (See 1 Peter 3:10). And preserve a spirit of love and so honor the Gospel of Christ.

4. For the lack of holiness and purity

> "Let no corrupt word proceed out of your mouth, but what is good for necessary edification, that it may impart grace to the hearers. And do not grieve the Holy Spirit of God, by whom you were sealed

for the day of redemption" (Ephesians 4:29-30).

If our conversations have offended the Spirit of God, it is clear that we will not be able to enjoy the Spirit of Prayer. We must always live conscious of His desires and surrender to the inner promptings of His Spirit. When He leads us in prayer, we must not grieve the Spirit by our disobedience, but rather we will leave all, preferring Him. There is nothing more important than to be in the presence of Christ and be used by Him to pray for lost souls. Let us lay aside with regularity, an hour daily to seek the face of God, and be very careful that nothing prevents us from following this custom If you hear the voice of the Spirit saying:

> "... Rise up, my love, my fair one, and come away!" (Songs of Solomon 2:13).

Even though it be in the middle of the night, pay attention to the voice of the Lord and obey the promptings of the Spirit. Maybe He wants to speak to you at that moment or warn you of some danger, and for that reason He is calling you to prayer.

We need to live continuously with God's peace in our hearts and his purity in our consciences "Beloved, if our heart does not condemn us, we have confidence toward God" (1 John 3:21). The Scripture also says:

> "Likewise the Spirit also helps in our weaknesses. For we do not know what we should pray for as we ought, but the

Spirit Himself makes intercession for us with groanings which cannot be uttered. Now He who searches the hearts knows what the mind of the Spirit is, because He makes intercession for the saints according to the will of God" (Romans 8:26-27).

Without holiness it is impossible to have the spirit of prayer, since the text evidently reveals that it is the saints who can experience His influence.

5. For the distractions and lack of perseverance

When one purposes in his heart to pray, the devil is sure to begin sending distractions. Since he knows how powerful a saint who prays in the Spirit is, his demons will do everything possible to obstruct and impede his prayers. They can come as thoughts or worries, or phone calls, or unexpected visitors who come to take your time and distract you from your purpose.

That is why Jesus said, "But you, when you pray, go into your room, and when you have shut your door, pray to your Father who is in the secret place" (Matthew 6:6). The "shut your door" shows us the importance to find a place and a time where we can seek God's face without interruptions or distractions and meditate on His Word.

The Spirit of Prayer

There are deliberate or willful distractions which, due to the lack of discipline in our lives, we allow to steal the Lord's time.

Another impediment to prayer is the lack of perseverance. The widow went to the unrighteous Judge, asking for Justice, she continued after him until he got wearied of her calls and he undertook her cause to defend her.

Jesus used that story to make a contrast between the unrighteous Judge and the Righteous and Merciful God. He did not compare him but used him as a contrast, saying that if the unrighteous Judge who did not fear God, nor regarded man, was moved to act because of the persistence of this woman, how much more will God avenge his children, from him who wants to rob us of our inheritance in Christ and of the benefits of Calvary. Here is the need to persevere in prayer until our prayers will penetrate the spiritual darkness and the answer comes.

"The effective, fervent prayer of a righteous man avails much" (James 5:16). This prayer in the Spirit, can soften the hearts and change situations, making possible the conversion of souls and breaking the resistance of the impenitent heart.

6. For grieving the Holy Spirit

Another impediment to prayer is when we have grieved the Holy Spirit "And do not grieve the Holy Spirit of God, by whom you were sealed for the day of redemption" (Ephesians 4:30).

The Spirit of Prayer

First of all we can grieve the Holy Spirit, by disobedience. Not only disobedience to God, but disobedience to the authority delegated by God: parents, pastors, leaders, husbands, etc. One can grieve the Spirit by vain conversations, by a flippant attitude, by being preoccupied with worldly things, by not paying attention to the promptings of the Spirit and by hardness of heart until you no longer feel the call of the Spirit to prayer.

The Spirit is also grieved by disagreements, arguments, shouting and by the lack of respect for one another. We are one body, and when we sin against the sensibility or conscience of a brother or family member, the Spirit, like a dove, withdraws. The symbols of the Holy Spirit are: The dove, the wind, the fire, the water and the blood. As the blood gives life to the body, so the Holy Spirit gives life to His body when Christ said:

> "Most assuredly, I say to you, unless you eat the flesh of the Son of Man and drink His blood, you have no life in you" (John 6:53).

Jesus was referring to drinking of His Spirit and eating of His Word. The Word made flesh. By not feeding ourselves and making use of the means of grace that God has provided, we are losing life and the desire to pray.

7. For unbelief

Another impediment to prayer is doubt, not believing that God listens or that God can and wants to intervene in our circumstances.

The Bible says:

> "But without faith it is impossible to please Him, for he who comes to God must believe that He is, and that He is a rewarder of those who diligently seek Him" (Hebrews 11:6).

> "Therefore I say to you, whatever things you ask when you pray, believe that you receive them, and you will have them" (Mark 11:24).

One loses strength and stops praying, when he sees no apparent results or at least no visible results. It is there that faith leaps beyond the chasm and leads us into the presence of God. Only prayer in the Spirit gives us the assurance that God hears us.

> "Now this is the confidence that we have in Him, that if we ask anything according to His will, He hears us. And if we know that He hears us, whatever we ask, we know that we have the petitions that we have asked of Him" (1 John 5:14,15).

By praying in the Spirit we can be sure that God hears us: "For through Him we both have access by one Spirit to the Father" (Ephesians 2:18).

The Spirit of Prayer

Examine yourself at the light of these truths and seek to not let another day pass without having the spirit of prayer.

God has promised it, you need it, the church awaits it, and God wants to grant it. "Be filled with the Spirit". Amen.

CHAPTER 8
THE GIFTS OF THE SPIRIT

"But the manifestation of the Spirit is given to each one for the profit of all: for to one is given the word of wisdom through the Spirit, to another the word of knowledge through the same Spirit, to another faith by the same Spirit, to another gifts of healings by the same Spirit, to another the working of miracles, to another prophecy, to another discerning of spirits, to another different kinds of tongues, to another the interpretation of tongues. But one and the same Spirit works all these things, distributing to each one individually as He wills" (1 Corinthians 12:7-11).

"Now concerning spiritual gifts, brethren, I do not want you to be ignorant" (1 Corinthians 12:1).

The will of God is that we know the things of the Spirit

It is the will of God that we should know the things of the Spirit that are given to us freely and that we understand about the operations of the gifts. There is a great ignorance prevailing in the Church concerning the gifts of the Spirit, despite the very clear explanations found in Scriptures.

The Gifts of the Spirit

The reason for this ignorance most certainly lies with the fact that "the natural man does not receive the things of the Spirit of God, for they are foolishness to him; nor can he know them, because they are spiritually discerned" (1 Corinthians 2:14).

I believe that the lack of knowledge about the operations of the gifts is one of the reasons for which they do not have their proper place in our meetings. There are some who for fear of excesses of fanaticism close their minds to what is true and reject the manifestations of the Spirit. In these last days, God is restoring the gifts of the Spirit and the power present in the early Church.

> "So I will restore to you the years that the swarming locust has eaten, the crawling locust, the consuming locust, And the chewing locust, My great army which I sent among you" (Joel 2:25).

Not only do we have the promise of the restoration of God's power in the Church, but also, in these last days God is doing and will do greater things than at the beginning. "'The glory of this latter temple shall be greater than the former, says the Lord of hosts" (Haggai 2:9).

God will send us the early and the latter rain. The restoration of the gifts of the Spirit and the great miracles and signs made in the Name of Jesus are a positive sign that the coming of our Lord is near. Jesus said: "And this gospel of the kingdom will be preached in all the world as a witness to all the

The Gifts of the Spirit

nations, and then the end will come" (Matthew 24:14).

The Holy Spirit brings the nine gifts and operates for the edification of the Church and for the benefit of each believer. "But the manifestation of the Spirit is given to each one for the profit of all" (1 Corinthians 12:7).

The gifts of the Spirit may be classified in three groups to supply the needs of the Church. These three categories are the gifts of expression, gifts of revelation and the gifts of power.

Gifts of Expression
- Prophecy.
- Different kinds of tongues.
- Interpretation of tongues.

Gifts of Revelation
- Word of Wisdom.
- Word of Knowledge.
- Discerning of spirits.

Gifts of Power
- Gift of faith.
- Gifts of healings (plural).
- Working of miracles.

All the gifts are operated by the Holy Spirit in the believer, as if he was an instrument for the manifestation of the gift.

The Gifts of the Spirit

The gifts are supernatural and operated by the Spirit always with the collaboration of the person.

The misconception, for example, that doctors have the gift of healing because they help the sick, is outside of what the Bible teaches us. There is no need for the manifestation of the Spirit in order to practice medicine or nursing. Thank God for them, but they are the product of teaching and science. The only medicine prescribed by the Bible is the anointing with oil in the name of the Lord, the laying on of hands and the prayer of faith.

Another discrepancy is to say that one endowed with a musical talent has the gift of music. These are natural gifts that God can use, but "the charisms" (or manifestations) of the Spirit are clearly described in the text.

Others speak of the gift of intercession, which is also not mentioned in the nine gifts. On the contrary, it is the obligation of every believer to pray in the Spirit "with all prayers and supplications".

The gifts are given by the Spirit and distributed to each one as He wills. It is God's will that we desire the gifts and seek the best gifts for the edification of the Body.

> "But earnestly desire the best gifts" (1 Corinthians 12:31).

The gifts of the Spirit are given to do the same works Christ has done

All the gifts of the Spirit were operating in the life and ministry of Christ because He was given the Spirit without measure. The Church, the mystical Body of Christ, must have the same gifts in operation and thus continue with the works that Christ began doing.

> "Most assuredly, I say to you, he who believes in Me, the works that I do he will do also; and greater works than these he will do, because I go to My Father" (John 14:12).

This promise is not only given to the Body of Christ (The Church), but this is a promise given individually to "he who believes". This promise is understood as being given when Jesus would go to the Father and then would give the Holy Spirit to the Church.

> "Nevertheless I tell you the truth. It is to your advantage that I go away; for if I do not go away, the Helper will not come to you; but if I depart, I will send Him to you" (John 16:7).

The secret to be able to do the same works and "greater works than these" consists in the coming of the Holy Spirit who is poured upon "all flesh" who receives Him. The Holy Spirit was confined to the body of Christ, but now He is everywhere. We, His disciples filled and guided by the Spirit, are His

The Gifts of the Spirit

voice, speaking the Word of God with authority and power. We must be His eyes, seeing the needs of humanity, and His ears, to listen with compassion to the voice of the afflicted. Our members must be presented to Him in living sacrifice, Holy and acceptable to God (See Romans 12:1) to do the works of healing and liberation which He operates through us.

The mystical body of Christ is composed of many members; each one has a function and his proper place in the ministry. Each member of the body must be filled with the Spirit, and fulfill his place in the body, taking part in the edification of others. Besides the gifts of the Spirit we have the fivefold ministerial gifts which are governmental gifts.

> "And he gave some, apostles; and some, prophets; and some, evangelists; and some, pastors and teachers; for the perfecting of the saints, for the work of the ministry, for the edifying of the body of Christ" (Ephesians 4:11,12)

> "Having then gifts differing according to the grace that is given to us, let us use them: if prophecy, let us prophesy in proportion to our faith; or ministry, let us use it in our ministering; he who teaches, in teaching; he who exhorts, in exhortation; he who gives, with liberality; he who leads, with diligence; he who shows mercy, with cheerfulness" (Romans 12:6-8).

The Gifts of the Spirit

I cannot imagine the possibility of having the gifts of the Spirit in operation without the initial experience of being baptized in the Holy Spirit, although the fruit of the Spirit may begin to be manifested with the new birth. When I speak of the gifts of the Spirit, the reader must not confuse the fruit of the Spirit with the fivefold ministry gifts given to the Church. (See Galatians 5:22-23).

- The *gifts or manifestations given by the Spirit* are: gift of the word of wisdom, gift of the word of knowledge, gift of faith, gifts of healing, gift of power of miracles, gift of prophecy, gift of discerning of spirits, gift of different kinds of tongues, gift of interpretation of tongues.

- Thus, the *fruit of the Spirit* with its nine characteristics: "But the fruit of the Spirit is love, joy, peace, longsuffering, kindness, goodness, faithfulness, gentleness, self-control. Against such there is no law" (Galatians 5:22-23).

- There are five *Ministries given to the Church by Christ:* Apostles, Prophets, Evangelists, Pastors and Teachers, and they are given "for the equipping of the saints for the work of ministry, for the edifying of the body of Christ" (Ephesians 4:12).

The manifold grace of God operates through His Spirit in endless manifestations to edify the Church, to do the work of evangelism and to supply the needs of people. God has no limits therefore He

The five Ministries in the Church

works through His people in many ways to benefit humanity.

Before going on with the theme of the gifts of the Spirit, we shall give a brief explanation of the five gift-ministries, in order to avoid confusion in further discourses.

> "There are diversities of gifts, but the same Spirit. There are differences of ministries, but the same Lord" (1 Corinthians 12:4-5).

Note the distinction between the gifts distributed by the Spirit and the ministries given by the Lord. The gift-ministries are an evidence of Christ working in His people.

> "And He (Jesus) Himself gave some to be *Apostles*, some *Prophets*, some *Evangelists*, and some *Pastors* and *Teachers*, for the equipping of the saints for the work of ministry, for the edifying of the body of Christ, till we all come to the unity of the faith and of the knowledge of the Son of God, to a perfect man, to the measure of the stature of the fullness of Christ" (Ephesians 4:11-13).

These ministry-gifts that are given for the perfecting of the Church, will be in her, until the day of the coming of the Lord, when we shall be raptured together with Him in the sky. It is very

The Gifts of the Spirit

easy to discern that the actual Church is still very far from the "measure of the stature of the fullness of Christ"; therefore it is necessary to have these ministries functioning in the Church.

These five gift ministries individually represent Christ in all his glory, caring for His Church to bring it to the unity of faith.

God has granted these gifts meant for the spiritual government in the Church. Not recognizing them has caused the Church in many instances to be divided and governed carnally. I cannot now deal with this subject in greater depth, but this is given so as to clarify the difference between the gifts of the Spirit and the ministries given to the Church by our Risen Lord.

The five ministerial gifts (apostles, prophets, evangelists, teachers and pastors) are men whom God has chosen, not by democratic vote or by their own will. They represent Christ to the Church. The Church simply recognizes what God has anointed and equipped. God sends them as His ambassadors and officers to put order in the ranks and prepare His army for battle. The one who shows respect to the officer honors the one who sent him. The one who puts apostolic ordinances into practice shows reverence for the head of the Church, Jesus Christ.

Saint Paul clarifies that the gifts of the Spirit will cease to be necessary when that which is perfect has come. "But when that which is perfect has come, then that which is in part will be done away" (1 Corinthians 13:10). What does perfect mean and when shall it come? It is clear that it is not now, rather something in the future.

"For now we see in a mirror, dimly, but then face to face" Now we do not see Jesus face to face, rather we live by faith, not by sight. "Now I know in part, but then I shall know just as I also am known" (1 Corinthians 13:12). God knows us perfectly, but as for us, we still have a long way to go to know Him. But one day we shall see Him face to face and this veil shall be taken away.

Therefore, the gifts of the Spirit, as: the word of knowledge, the word of wisdom, prophecy, tongues and interpretation, etc. are necessary for us to better understand God's mind. Because His thoughts are not our thoughts, rather the Holy Spirit reveals them to us when it is necessary and when He wants. What shall we do then? "... earnestly desire the best gifts." (1 Corinthians 12:31).

The gifts of the Spirit and their function in the mystical body of Christ

> "How is it then, brethren? Whenever you come together, each of you has a psalm, has a teaching, has a tongue, has a revelation, has an interpretation. Let all things be done for edification" (1 Corinthians 14:26).

The Gifts of the Spirit

God's plan for the Church is for each member to have their ministry and that each person participates in the building up of the others. In the building up of the spiritual Church, the builder has a place for every "living stone" in the edification of this temple for a habitation of the Spirit. "you also, as living stones, are being built up a spiritual house, a holy priesthood, to offer up spiritual sacrifices acceptable to God through Jesus Christ" (1 Peter 2:5).

In the text we have read that "each of you" must have his part in the operation of the gifts given to us.

We may have the situation, that by having too many members present, not everyone may be able to participate in every Service. In this case, he who presides must keep the order under the guidance of the Spirit. Let us trust in the intelligence of the omniscient Spirit to order and direct through the presiding minister, if this one is full of the Spirit.

Having different gifts according to the Grace that has been given to us, we must use the gifts according to the measure of faith, for the Glory of God. When I speak of "gifts", the reader must understand I am not referring to natural gifts or talents, but supernatural gifts of the Spirit. As in our physical bodies all our members operate for the benefit of the body, so must it be in the Church, the mystical body of Christ. In the physical body, the mind governs the actions of the body and everything is coordinated for the health and benefit of the body. In an impaired or paralyzed person, the sick members do not operate according to the impulses sent from the head; and due to the sickness, they do not receive the impulses from the nerves.

The Church has for its head Jesus Christ and receives the commandments sent by Christ through His Spirit. "... Christ is head of the Church; and He is the Savior of the Body" (Ephesians 5:23). Christ sustains and cares for the Church because we are members of His Body, of His flesh and of his bones. "For as the body is one and has many members, but all the members of that one body, being many, are one body, so also is Christ" (1 Corinthians 12:12).

In several aspects, the Church today, being divided by bitterness, envy and false doctrines, is sick and without power. The Scripture exhorts us: "endeavoring to keep the unity of the Spirit in the bond of peace" (Ephesians 4:3). For the lack of being full of the Spirit, the Church has been led by carnal leaders and instead of being a healthy and strong body; it sometimes looks like a political machine. I am not saying that the mystical body of Christ is divided and sick; it is the Church we see with our natural eyes. The mystical body of Christ is perfect and glorious, sanctified by the washing of water by the Word until it be a Church without spot or wrinkle. Even in the midst of the apostasy and falling away of the present day! Christ has His Church, controlled by His Spirit and indivisible in Love. I do not believe that the true Church would

The Gifts of the Spirit

become a visible organization under a human head as of a world church. Rather, when we see this happening, we can be very sure that it is the antichrist, whose coming is after the working of Satan. I believe God can use the various denominations in His plan to unite them in one body, and that every denomination that would have the fundamental doctrines correct, may enter in God's plan.

What separates and divides the brethren are the prejudice and lack of the love of God. We should not see the unity of the body of Christ as a world church, rather as a spiritual unity, that is manifested by the love of God. In His prayer Christ said:

> "That they all may be one, as you, Father, are in me, and I in you; that they also may be one in us, that the world may believe that you sent me" (John 17:21).

The unity Christ enjoyed with the Father was not physical, but spiritual; God in Him and Him in God. The unity the Church must have, will not necessarily be physical, rather the unity that we have as members of one another, united in the same spirit and the same love. We have become a part of the mystical body of Christ, not by merely being members of a local church, but by being born again in the family of God by the Spirit.

> "For by one Spirit we were all baptized into one body ... and have all been made to drink into one Spirit" (1 Corinthians

12:13).

The baptism referred here is the spiritual baptism into the mystical and invisible body of Christ, which occurs at the moment we believe and are born again.

By receiving Christ as our only and sufficient Savior, we are participants of the family of God, joint heirs with Christ Jesus. The second phrase says we "have been all made to drink into one Spirit". This refers to the baptism of the Spirit.

> "But as many as received Him, to them He gave the right to become children of God, to those who believe in His name: who were born, not of blood, nor of the will of the flesh, nor of the will of man, but of God" (John 1:12,13).

We must recognize our union with the head (Christ) and our unity one with another. If we are baptized in the body of Christ by faith, we are members of his flesh and of his bones, and it is to our advantage that we love one another, despite our small differences. "That there should be no schism in the body, but that the members should have the same care for one another" (1 Corinthians 12:25).

The gift of different kinds of tongues

Before addressing the explanation of the gift of "different kinds of tongues", it is necessary to clarify the difference between the gift of different kinds of tongues and the tongues as evidence or sign that we have received the baptism in the Holy Spirit.

Not all those who speak in tongues have the gift of "different kinds of tongues". When the Spirit comes to dwell in the believer by the Baptism in the Spirit, the initial manifestation is the speaking in tongues and that can be accompanied by prophecy. "And when Paul had laid hands on them, the Holy Spirit came upon them, and they spoke with tongues and prophesied" (Acts 19:6). He shows His presence by speaking, using our faculties and our tongue.

After the initial Baptism in the Holy Spirit, the believer must speak in tongues in his personal devotions, to edify himself and to speak mysteries in the Spirit.

When Saint Paul asks: Do all speak with tongues? he does not refer to speaking in tongues in prayer, nor as the evidence of baptism received, but to the gift of different kinds of tongues. This gift must be used in the Church together with the gift of interpretation of tongues for the body (the Church) to receive edification.

To speak in an unknown tongue is very necessary and beneficial as the Scripture says: "For he who speaks in a tongue does not speak to men but to God, for no one understands him; however, in the spirit he speaks mysteries" (1 Corinthians 14:2). Praying in tongues is like a direct line of the Spirit in us to God and gives growth and spiritual strength to the one who prays in tongues.

The Gifts of the Spirit

> "He who speaks in a tongue edifies himself... For if I pray in a tongue, my spirit prays... What is the conclusion then? I will pray with the spirit, and I will also pray with the understanding" (1 Corinthians 14:4,14,15).

So, speaking in tongues is to speak to God in the spirit, to speak mysteries, to build one self up, and to be used in the Church together with the gift of interpretation of tongues.

Saint Paul wrote, "Though I speak with the tongues of men and of angels, but have not love, I have become sounding brass or a clanging cymbal" (1 Corinthians 13:1).

In the previous chapter the apostle gives us the list of the gifts, including the gift of the different kinds of tongues as a manifestation of the Spirit. We understand that tongues are divided in two categories, humans and angelic. On the day of Pentecost, human tongues were heard; each one heard speaking in their own tongues the wonderful works of God. "Cretans and Arabs--we hear them speaking in our own tongues the wonderful works of God" (Acts 2:11).

We must differentiate between tongues as the sign of the baptism, and the tongues as a gift manifested together with the gift of interpretation of tongues.

1. Tongues as a sign:

"And these signs will follow those who believe: In My name they will cast out demons; they will speak with new tongues" (Mark 16:17).

2. Tongues for edification of the Church:
"Therefore let him who speaks in a tongue pray that he may interpret" (1 Corinthians 14:13).

Have tongues ceased?

For those who cling to the text in 1 Corinthians 13:8 where it states that "tongues, they will cease"; these propose "that which is perfect" to which Saint Paul is referring is the end of tongues when the Bible was finished writing.

> "... But whether there are prophecies, they will fail; whether there are tongues, they will cease; whether there is knowledge, it will vanish away. For we know in part and we prophesy in part. But when that which is perfect has come, then that which is in part will be done away" (1 Corinthians 13:8-10).

This argument has no Biblical nor logical basis. Saint Paul in verse 12 says: "For now we see in a mirror, dimly, but then face to face. Now I know in part, but then I shall know just as I also am known". When shall this be? Not in this life, rather when we shall see him and shall be like Him, knowing as we are known.

Jesus giving the signs of the believer until the end of the world said: "And these signs will follow those

The Gifts of the Spirit

who believe: In My name they will cast out demons; they will speak with new tongues". In this same text He speaks of the baptism in water: "And He said to them, Go into all the world and preach the gospel to every creature. He who believes and is baptized will be saved; but he who does not believe will be condemned" (Mark 16:15-16).

Since we continue baptizing in water, Why not the other? That is to say: Why not continue to speak in tongues as a sign until the end? Saint Paul said, "do not forbid to speak with tongues" (1 Corinthians 14:39). In some churches, they will throw you out if you do.

But Saint Paul also says that if there are no interpreters of the message in tongues, let him speak with himself, i.e., let him not manifest it in public (1 Corinthians 14:28). It also says that if there were present uninformed or unbelievers, that are people who do not understand spiritual things, they will think that you are out of your mind. Does this mean that it is forbidden to give a message in tongues? Absolutely not! But it does say that everything should be done decently and in order. Let it be done, not cancelled, but in order. "Let all things be done decently and in order" (1 Corinthians 14:40).

Children need to learn obedience and discipline, the spiritual children as well.

Amongst other gifts mentioned in 1 Corinthians 12, is the gift of tongues. We cannot accept the gifts

The Gifts of the Spirit

that one wants and reject the others. The order in a Service is clear. "How is it then, brethren? Whenever you come together, each of you has a psalm, has a teaching, has a tongue, has a revelation, has an interpretation. Let all things be done for edification" (1 Corinthians 14:26).

If upon the finishing of writing the Scriptures and the emphasis on love (1 Corinthians 13). Gifts are no more. Why does Saint Paul after speaking of love, as the perfecting of the spiritual life, in chapter 13, continue by saying in chapter 14 "Pursue love, and desire spiritual gifts, but especially that you may prophesy".

The gift of tongues with the gift of interpretation of tongues is equivalent to prophecy. Here the apostle makes emphasis on the edification of the Church and the superiority of the gift of prophecy over the gift of tongues. (1 Corinthians 14:5 and 12).

The preaching of the word and the gift of prophecy are different, and we must not twist the Bible to justify the absence of the gifts. The gift of prophecy for edification is spontaneous, given at that moment for:

- Strengthening (edification).
- Encourage (exhortation).
- Comfort (comfort).

What then is the use of tongues today?
1. First as a sign for unbelievers (1 Corinthians 14:22).

2. As a sign of the Baptism in the Holy Spirit (Acts 10:45-46).
3. To strengthen and build up him who speaks (1 Corinthians 14:4).
4. To pray in the Spirit (1 Corinthians 14:15).
5. To sing in the Spirit (1 Corinthians 14:16).

A message in tongues together with the gift of interpretation of tongues confirms the word preached, and never is a substitute to the preaching. The ministerial gifts are: apostles, prophets, evangelists, pastors and teachers and they are above in authority to the gifts of the Spirit.

If this truth was understood, many mistakes would be avoided in the Church. For example, raising someone who has a gift of knowledge or healing above the ministerial gifts and receiving everything that comes out of his mouth as the Word of God. The Church is founded upon the ministry of the apostles and prophets, not upon the charismatic gifts.

During the more than sixty years that I am in the Church, I have seen so many disorders and mistakes due to this reason. The Bible must be taken as a whole and the New Testament as rules and regulations for today until the end of this dispensation. Not picking what you like and leaving the rest. The plans of the architect are made; let us beware how we build upon them.

Due to our lack of commitment and faith, we have been impoverished and instead of correcting our

The Gifts of the Spirit

walk, we try to change the Bible. But he who adds or he who takes away from the Scriptures is in danger of judgment. And what do we do with the abuses and disorders that we see in the churches who profess being filled with the Spirit? Simply we shed light and we correct what is deficient and it is set in order. We do not put aside the gifts that God has given because of some undisciplined persons who do not obey the word.

The gifts of the Spirit are not indicative of super-spirituality in those who have them, but rather of the mercy of God who wants to equip His Church.

Soldiers are taught to use weapons before being sent to war. God's weapons are not toys, but something God has given for spiritual warfare and for the edification of the Church.

Others ask, "And what about the scripture: they will take up serpents, is it for today?" Clearly God does not want us to tempt him by taking up serpents. Rather that if in any circumstances we are bitten by a serpent or drink anything deadly by mistake, we can have God's protection as Saint Paul had it, when a venomous serpent bit him and he shook it off in the fire, without suffering any harm.

Christ also said "You shall tread upon serpents and scorpions" referring to evil spirits who hide themselves and bite the careless and the one whose feet are not shod with the preparation of the

Gospel. We need to see how the apostles understood this before we come to conclusions.

We must have discernment together with the gifts of expression and judge the manifestation of tongues as well as the prophecies. We cannot prevent abuses and mistakes, but yes, we must teach the correct use of what God has given and separate the precious from the vile. Amen.

Tongues as evidence of the Baptism

With the coming of the Spirit on the day of Pentecost, the gifts were poured out on the believers. The gift of tongues accompanied the initial outpouring of the Holy Spirit, when by spontaneous utterances, the Holy Spirit spoke to the Jews gathered, fulfilling Joel's and Isaiah's prophecies.

> "And they were all filled with the Holy Ghost, and began to speak with other tongues, as the Spirit gave them utterance" (Acts 2:4)

In Cornelius' house we also find the manifestation of tongues as evidence.

> "And they of the circumcision which believed were astonished, as many as came with Peter, because that on the Gentiles also was poured out the gift of the Holy Ghost. For they heard them speak with tongues and magnify God" (Acts 10:45-46).

The Gifts of the Spirit

The believers in Samaria spoke in tongues upon receiving the Holy Spirit. Though no specific mention is made in this portion of the Scripture, we can still deduct that there were visible manifestations. "Then they laid hands on them, and they received the Holy Spirit. And when Simon saw that through the laying on of the apostles hands the Holy Spirit was given, he offered them money" (Acts 8:17-18).

Let us note that Saint Paul received the Holy Spirit through the laying on of the hands of Ananias, and though the evidence of unknown tongues is not mentioned, Paul confirms in his epistle. "I thank my God I speak with tongues more than you all" (1 Corinthians 14:18).

Twenty-three years after the day of Pentecost, we find the mention of the sign of tongues and of prophecy, when The Holy Spirit came down in Ephesus. "And when Paul had laid hands on them, the Holy Spirit came upon them, and they spoke with tongues and prophesied" (Acts 19:6).

Through these examples mentioned in Scriptures, we can positively conclude that the sign of speaking in tongues must accompany the Baptism in the Holy Spirit. Besides Scriptures, I have the experience of having seen multitudes baptized in the Holy Spirit and all spoke in tongues as the Spirit gave them utterance. Some delay clearly speaking in tongues after receiving the Holy Spirit, but this should not be the norm, rather the exception.

The gift of different kinds of tongues and its operation in the Church

Let us now deal with the gift of different kinds of tongues, or messages in tongues. This gift together with the gift of interpretation of tongues is for the edification of the Church, that is to say, to confirm the preaching and to give a spontaneous message to the people.

Different kinks of tongues are supernatural expressions given by the Spirit through the believer and for the edification of the Church. This gift is given through the will of the Spirit and bestowed as He wills for the profit of all. For this cause Saint Paul asks: "Do all speak with tongues?"

Not all have the gift of different kinds of tongues because the text declares:

> "... To another different kinds of tongues, to another the interpretation of tongues. But one and the same Spirit works all these things, distributing to each one individually as he wills" (1 Corinthians 12:10,11).

Though the gift of different kinds of tongues is not given to all, tongues as a sign are for every believer, just as declared by Jesus' last words. "And these signs will follow those who believe: In My name they will cast out demons; they will speak with new tongues" (Mark 16:17). The spiritual expressions in tongues must be exercised regularly in our prayers, as we see very clearly through Scriptures.

The Gifts of the Spirit

The gift of "Different kinds of tongues" includes languages known of *men,* and *angelic* tongues, or spiritual tongues. When Saint Paul mentions the need for love in the exercise of the gifts, he declares: "Though I speak with the tongues of men and of angels, but have not love, I have become sounding brass or a clanging cymbal" (1 Corinthians 13:1). Whether they be tongues of man or angelic tongues, in both cases they are not understood by the one who speaks. They are unknown tongues.

When the person who speaks during a spontaneous message of the Spirit, expresses himself in a known tongue and understood by him, it is the gift of prophecy which is being manifested. On the day of Pentecost, God used human tongues to make his wonders manifest to all the Jews who had gathered in Jerusalem for the feast of Pentecost. "And when this sound occurred, the multitude came together, and were confused, because everyone heard them speak in his own language" (Acts 2:6). Saint Paul refers to angelic tongues when he said: "Therefore if the whole church comes together in one place, and all speak with tongues, and there come in those who are uninformed or unbelievers, will they not say that you are out of your mind?" (1 Corinthians 14:23). Here we can observe that the tongues referred to were unknown or angelic, because the unbelievers could not understand them.

The rule to operate the gifts of the Spirit in the Church is "to excel for the edification of the

The Gifts of the Spirit

Church". All the gifts must be operated decently and in order. The gift of different kinds of tongues is the expression of the Holy Spirit expressing a spiritual message for the *edification* and *exhortation*. As I stated earlier, not every manifestation of tongues is a message, it can also be the evidence of the baptism in the Spirit or a prayer in the Spirit, or praise or a spiritual song.

The gift of different kinds of tongues must be operated together with the gift of interpretation of tongues in order to be able to understand the intention or the meaning of the message given in the unknown tongue.

Let us note that it is not necessarily the *"translation"* of what was spoken in tongues, rather the *"interpretation"* or in other words, the meaning of the message in tongues. He that has the gift of different kinds of tongues is mandated by God, to pray for the gift of interpretation of tongues so that the church may be edified.

> "Therefore let him who speaks in a tongue pray that he may interpret" (1 Corinthians 14:13).

Thus we see that a person can have more than one gift operating in him, as the need arises. If the person who has the gift of different kinds of tongues does not have the gift of interpretation of tongues and knows for sure that no one else present has that gift, then the person is exhorted to keep silent.

The Gifts of the Spirit

"But if there is no interpreter, let him keep silent in church, and let him speak to himself and to God" (1 Corinthians 14:28).

The messages in tongues in a Service must not be more than three. "If anyone speaks in a tongue, let there be two or at the most three, each in turn, and let one interpret" (1 Corinthians 14:27). When the anointing of the Spirit comes upon someone, it is always to benefit and to edify. The believer exercising the gifts must seek the mind of the Spirit to know the will of the Spirit and not waste the anointing in a mere emotion. From experience the believer can find out whether the anointing is to exercise a gift, to pray, or to worship in the Spirit.

When the anointing comes upon the believer to exercise a gift, let him or her stand on his feet, thus receive the attention of the one who is leading the Service, as well as his permission to go ahead or wait, and then give his message in tongues, prophecy, etc. It is so because the gifts must be submitted to the five ministerial gifts. In that way, if the minister is preaching or in the middle of some teaching, he may finish his thought and give place to the message of the Spirit.

The others in the church must wait with attention and in silence, while the message is being delivered. The gift of interpretation of tongues must always follow the gift of different kinds of tongues and it cannot precede it. If the interpretation is not

The Gifts of the Spirit

forthcoming within the next minutes, then the Service must go on.

The gift of different kinds of tongues, in union with the gift of interpretation of tongues, is equal in importance to the gift of prophecy. "I wish you all spoke with tongues, but even more that you prophesied; for he who prophesies is greater than he who speaks with tongues, unless indeed he interprets, that the church may receive edification" (1 Corinthians 14:5).

In all the manifestations of the gifts, it is necessary to remind ourselves that we are exhorted not to quench nor grieve the Holy Spirit.

The Holy Spirit must have the preeminence in all our services and we must provide sufficient time for the gifts to be exercised. When the services or meetings are done with excessive concern with formalism and filled with rituals, it is very possible to grieve the Spirit. If the services are planned before hand in such a way as to not give freedom to the Spirit, it is quite likely that the gifts will never come into operation. When the ministers plan the meeting so strictly, filling every part, then the other gifts represented in the Service will not have the freedom of expression.

The nature of the Spirit is represented in the Bible as a dove, so gentle that He does not demand attention, but waits that His Presence be invited and sought. The gifts operate in the atmosphere of love, worship, and praise, and we must allow for

The Gifts of the Spirit

sufficient time in each Service for spiritual worship. Let us not forget that the same Paul who exhorted "...the spirits of the prophets are subject to the prophets" (1 Corinthians 14:32). Also said: "Therefore, brethren, desire earnestly to prophesy, and do not forbid to speak with tongues" (1 Corinthians 14:39). I have given here the order for normal Services, but there will be exceptions in special Services.

The gift of Prophecy

"Pursue love, and desire spiritual gifts, but especially that you may prophesy" (1 Corinthians 14:1).

Prophecy is the expression in a known tongue, divinely inspired and spontaneous. As the different kinds of tongues, so prophecy is the expression of the Spirit in a tongue known by the one who prophecies. The will and faith of the person who prophecies are active in the prophecy; he who exercises this gift is merely an instrument for the Spirit to express Himself. The Spirit of God needs a body to express Himself and lips to speak His divine words. When Christ was on the earth in the form of a man, He spoke the words that He heard from the Father, "He is the image of the invisible God, ... For in Him dwells all the fullness of the Godhead bodily;" (Colossians 1:15; 2:9). Before ascending to the Father, Christ promised the Holy Spirit, who would speak what He would hear from the Father.

"However, when He, the Spirit of truth,

The Gifts of the Spirit

has come, He will guide you into all truth; for He will not speak on His own authority, but whatever He hears He will speak; and He will tell you things to come" (John 16:13).

One of the ways that the Spirit speaks to us is through the gift of prophecy.

It is needful to note that the gift of prophecy is not the same as the preaching of the Word, nor is it the same as the ministry of the prophet. As we have already said, the ministry of prophet is one of the five ministries given by Christ to the Church, and it is not one of the nine gifts of the Spirit.

The gift of prophecy is firstly for the edification (spiritual growth), exhortation, and comfort. "But he who prophesies speaks edification and exhortation and comfort to men" (1 Corinthians 14:3). Though in some sense, the objective of prophecy is the same as preaching, yet they are not the same. The gift of prophecy is operated by the Spirit, when He wants and not by the will of man. Besides, the thoughts projected to the one who prophecies, cannot be planned as those of a sermon, rather they are *spontaneous* expressions of the Spirit.

Besides edification, exhortation, and comfort, the gift of prophecy is used by God to convict of sin.

"But if all prophesy, and an unbeliever or an uninformed person comes in, he is

The Gifts of the Spirit

convinced by all, he is convicted by all" (1 Corinthians 14:24).

The omniscient Spirit of God knows every heart and every thought, and He can reveal through the gift of prophecy what is hidden. "And thus the secrets of his heart are revealed; and so, falling down on his face, he will worship God and report that God is truly among you" (1 Corinthians 14:25).

Truths that have not yet been revealed, but are in the mind of God, can be made known by prophecy and thus can exhort and teach the believers. "For you can all prophesy one by one, that all may learn and all may be encouraged." (1 Corinthians 14:31).

The number of prophecies in a service is also revealed to us, being of two or three. "Let two or three prophets speak, and let the others judge" (1 Corinthians 14:29). This applies also to the gift of tongues and interpretation of tongues. When the Scripture says: "you can all prophesy one by one", it does not refer to within the scope of one service, rather that all will have the opportunity to prophesy as they are chosen by the Spirit in the future meetings. Besides, when Saint Paul refers to "you can all prophesy" he refers to those who have the gift of prophecy and not to all in the church; he simply states that all with the gift of prophecy will have their opportunity to prophecy and they should not all try to exercise their gift within a single service, but rather only two or three. In some occasion it may appear that there are more than three messages in tongues and interpretations, or

The Gifts of the Spirit

more than three prophecies; nonetheless it can be that the message or the prophecy may be incomplete, requiring thus to be completed by means of another person; this makes that one and the same message may be given in two parts.

Each prophecy must be judged by the others who prophecy and must always be in accord with the Bible in words and meaning. I do not say these must sit as in a tribunal to judge, but in spirit, we must discern if this is the mind of the Holy Spirit or not. If it has not been the mind of the Holy Spirit, then the true message must be given. The gift of prophecy is not for adding to the Scriptures, because the Bible is the full counsel of God.

Prophecy can shed light on the Scriptures or reveal the spiritual condition that exists in the church. The fundamental doctrines of the Church must proceed exclusively from the Holy Bible. The expressions of the gifts are revelations or exhortations based on the Word and not modern revelations nor add-ons to the Word of God. The gift of prophecy must not be used to direct lives nor to predict the future. This is very important!!!

The ministry of the prophet (Ephesians 4:11), is deeper than the gift of prophecy, and is used to direct, reveal the future and to separate believers for the ministry. (See 1 Timothy 1:18 and 4:14; Acts 21:11 and 13:1.2). Study well these scriptures so that you may be able to distinguish between the ministry of prophet, and the limitation of the gift of prophecy.

The Gifts of the Spirit

Notice the order of authority in the ministry gifts: first apostles, second prophets, thirdly teachers and so on.

> "And God hath set some in the church, first apostles, secondarily prophets, thirdly teachers, after that miracles, then gifts of healings, helps, governments, diversities of tongues" (1 Corinthians 12:28).

Now concerning the gift of prophecy, which is different than the ministry of the prophet – the gift of prophecy in someone may be much more limited than in another person.

The revelations given through the gifts to a person may be greater than in another believer. The depth of the gift of prophecy depends much on the knowledge of the individual and his measure of faith. "Having then gifts differing according to the grace that is given to us, let us use them: if prophecy, let us prophesy in proportion to our faith" (Romans 12:6).

The gift of the Word of Knowledge

> "For to one is given the word of wisdom through the Spirit, to another the word of knowledge through the same Spirit" (1 Corinthians 12:8).

The gift of the word of knowledge is a supernatural revelation of a fact or truth in the mind of God revealed to the believer by the Spirit. It is needful to

The Gifts of the Spirit

point that it is not the gift of knowledge, but of the word of knowledge. Only God is omniscient and has all the treasures of knowledge hidden in Him. When in His Divine wisdom, He wants to impart to his children a word of knowledge, He ministers this gift.

The gift of the word of knowledge is operated when God sees there is a need and that we are in the spiritual condition to receive it. This gift is not necessarily an oral gift but a revelation to the person; the person may speak it out or not, according to the need.

This gift was manifested in the prophets of old. For example, it was revealed in the life and ministry of Elisha. "Then Elisha said, Hear the word of the Lord. Thus says the Lord: Tomorrow about this time a seah of fine flour shall be sold for a shekel, and two seahs of barley for a shekel, at the gate of Samaria" (2 Kings 7:1). By the word of knowledge, God could reveal to his servant, the fact that the famine present was going to cease and that abundance would come through a miracle.

The gift of the word of knowledge was operated in Him when by the Spirit he saw (in the Spirit) his servant Gehazi follow Naaman and ask him for clothing. (See 2 Kings 5:26). By the gift of the word of knowledge, the prophet Samuel revealed to Saul that his donkeys which had been lost were now found. (See 1 Samuel 10:1-2).

The Gifts of the Spirit

This gift also manifested in the life and ministry of Christ. An indisputable example of this gift operating in Christ is found in the calling of Nathanael. "Jesus saw Nathanael coming toward Him, and said of him, Behold, an Israelite indeed, in whom is no deceit! Nathanael said to Him, how do You know me? Jesus answered and said to him, Before Philip called you, when you were under the fig tree, I saw you" (John 1:47-48). By a revelation of the Spirit, Christ saw Nathanael under the fig tree and knew his character and his heart. You may think that being God in the form of a man, Christ knew all things. Christ referred to himself as the "son of man".

The temptation in the wilderness had the purpose to move him to act as God, "If You are the Son of God, command that these stones become bread" (Matthew 4:3).

Jesus refused to operate as God in the flesh, limiting himself to operate in the Spirit. When he was arrested in the garden of Gethsemane, He did not use His divine power to free himself, rather he said to Peter: "Or do you think that I cannot now pray to My Father, and He will provide Me with more than twelve legions of angels?" (Matthew 26:53). He acted as a man filled with the Spirit and for this reason He could say: "Most assuredly, I say to you, he who believes in Me, the works that I do he will do also; and greater works than these he will do" (John 14:12). God has provided the gifts of the word of knowledge and the word of wisdom so

The Gifts of the Spirit

that in the opportune moment, He may reveal part of His mind to His children.

The works Christ did, He promised that His disciples were also going to do. The gifts which were operating without limits in Christ, can operate in us according to our measure of faith. The possibilities offered to us by Christ, sometimes transcend our knowledge and understanding. The majority of us, live below the aim we may obtain by the knowledge of the purposes of God. We are limited by our lack of faith and spiritual vision, but with God there are no limitations. "all things are possible to him who believes" (Mark 9:23).

And nothing shall be impossible for us if we believe it from the heart.

The gift of the word of knowledge is operated in various ministers today, together with the gift of healings. By the word of knowledge, the sicknesses and problems are revealed, thus inspiring faith for the healing. Nathanael believed in Christ as the Messiah by the manifestation of this gift and today still, this gift reveals truths known only by God, to bring souls to the knowledge of Christ. By this gift, Peter was able to reveal the deceit of Ananias and Sapphira when these deceived about the price of the land they sold.

> "But Peter said, Ananias, why has Satan filled your heart to lie to the Holy Spirit and keep back part of the price of the land for yourself?" (Acts 5:3).

The Gifts of the Spirit

By the operation of this gift, great fear came to the whole church and the result was that "And believers were increasingly added to the Lord, multitudes of both men and women" (Acts 5:14). Paul also while preaching in certain occasion, understood by the word of knowledge that a certain man had faith to be healed.

> "This man heard Paul speaking. Paul, observing him intently and seeing that he had faith to be healed, said with a loud voice, Stand up straight on your feet! And he leaped and walked" (Acts 14:9-10).

Only by the revelation of the Spirit, Saint Paul could see the faith in the cripple, because faith is not seen with natural eyes. By the word of knowledge, Paul could reveal deep mysteries hidden from the foundation of the world. In many occasions this gift is operated jointly with the gift of the word of wisdom, for the edification of the church.

The gift of the Word of Wisdom

The gift of the Word of Wisdom in the same way as the gift of the Word of Knowledge does not reveal all wisdom but as it says, it is a word, of wisdom. This gift is always a supernatural one and must never be confused with human wisdom, nor with the wisdom we receive by scrutinizing the Scriptures. Rather it is a Word of Wisdom sent by God to the mind and heart like a ray of light so that the servant of God can be equipped in the time of

The Gifts of the Spirit

necessity. When our wisdom is insufficient, God can give us the Word of Wisdom.

To make this clearer we can say that the Word of Wisdom is the wisdom of God which is revealed through this gift in order that we may use the knowledge received through the Word of Knowledge. I can give you an example from my own life showing how these gifts function in practice. While I was attending a church in Florida just as a member of the congregation, I listened to a woman singing a solo. She was of Greek origin and her mother was a member of the Greek Orthodox Church. She was a very likable woman and always seemed happy.

While I was praying, the Lord revealed to me through the word of knowledge that she had an adulterous relationship with the head of the firm where she worked.

I went to her house with the conviction that I had to tell her of the danger she was in. Once we had started our conversation I tried to see if she wanted to open up and seek help. As always she looked very happy as if there were no problem. She had a perfect camouflage with her permanent smile. In the end I had no choice but to tell her clearly what I felt God was saying and risk the possible outcome. On hearing this word of God she was truly amazed and started racking her mind as to who could possibly have revealed this to me, and she asked frightened: "Who told you?" I assured her that no one had told me, but that God had revealed it to me.

Also, together with the Word of Knowledge, God gave me the Word of Wisdom for her and I had a clear reply as to how she could get out of this tangle. It was by this Word of wisdom that I was able to state the solution that God had given me for her problem and how she could be set free from this snare of Satan. She was so tied by the desires of the flesh and so impoverished spiritually that she could not escape. The Lord showed me that if she repented and fasted for four days that He would break the power of this physical attraction that was holding her in bondage and so she would be set free. Also the Lord made it known to her that she was to leave her work for that was the origin of the problem.

She made excuses, saying that her mother was going to visit her and therefore she couldn't fast although the truth of the matter was she was not prepared to give up this relationship. I came to know later that she was divorced and that she separated from the Lord. Her sin cost her soul but God in His omniscience had warned her beforehand.

This gift operated with Elisha when he sent a messenger to Naaman telling him: "Wash in the Jordan seven times and your flesh shall be restored to you and you shall be clean" (2 Kings 5:10). It seems, the Word of Knowledge was operating, but I think the Word of Wisdom of God revealed to Elisha

The Gifts of the Spirit

the pride of Naaman and because of that he had to be washed before the healing could come. The shame of having to go down to the muddy stream of the Jordan shook the egoism of this famous man, until the seventh time of his immersion in the water, then God was able to heal him. In dealing with souls nowadays it is necessary to do this same thing and perceive where the lies hide. We have to get rid of all the hideouts of lies and demonstrate to people their selfishness, worldliness and any other thing that is opposed to God.

This gift was always operating in the life of Christ for He is the "Wisdom of God."

> "But to them which are called, both Jews and Greeks, Christ is the power of God, and the wisdom of God" (1 Corinthians 1:24).

A case that illustrates the operation of this gift is that of the adulterous woman brought before Christ. "So when they continued asking him, he got up, and said to them: He that is without sin among you, let him first cast a stone at her" (John 8:7). By this Word of Wisdom Christ rescued the woman from a cruel death and revealed God's Love which is great in forgiveness, and at the same time reprimanded sin in the Pharisees and Scribes. Also, Stephen, full of faith, and the Holy Spirit reprimanded the Jews in such a way... "and they stopped their ears, and ran upon him with one accord. And cast him out of the city and stoned him" (Acts 7:57-58). The Bible declares that they

The Gifts of the Spirit

stoned him because "they were not able to resist the wisdom and the Spirit by which he spoke" (Acts 6:10).

The Lord can manifest His will in various ways and not only by the gifts of revelation. These gifts operate when we have used up our own knowledge and wisdom and are in need of a supernatural revelation. We must remember that not everyone has these gifts but they are distributed to each person in accordance with God's will. The Lord can reveal His will through His word (see 2 Timothy 3:16) or through visions (see Acts 9:10 and 23:11) or through dreams (see Matthew 2:12) or through the Holy Spirit in us (see John 16:13). We must not just hope that God will speak to us through a spiritual gift and neglect to search for His will through His Word. We must live in the Spirit and thus we shall be guided by the Spirit into all Truth.

The difference between a Word of Knowledge and a Word of Wisdom

I have learned over the years that there exists a big difference between the gift of the word of knowledge and the gift of the word of wisdom. Nowadays there are many who exercise the gift of knowledge in what is termed: "a word from the Lord". Of course, God does speak through prophecies, but we have to proceed with great care in this matter since many wish to know their future and be acquainted with their spiritual state and these supposed gifts of knowledge nearly always tell them what they long

The Gifts of the Spirit

to hear and they go away "edified" or possibly "deceived".

I believe strongly in the exercise of all the gifts, but in this area of the spiritual world, discernment is required and above all we must judge everything in the light of the scriptures. God can speak and does speak through the gift of the word of knowledge but this is not a substitute for hearing the voice of God through His word and through the spiritual authorities, God has placed over you. One must take care with those who come from outside and who have the "gift of prophecy" and do not know the person concerned and this combined with the desire of leaving a good impression runs the risk that they may be mistaken if they are not really guided by the Holy Spirit. If the word they give is not of God, it can bring chaos and conflict not only in the person but in the Church.

I advise you to not only seek to have a confirmation in your own spirit, but also to submit this word to be judged by your authorities and those who are close to you who know you well. Be careful with prophecies that puff up the flesh, but avoid the cross. The way of the cross is the way of the Spirit.

But I return to the thought I want to make quite clear, that is, the considerable difference that exists in practice between the word of knowledge and the word of wisdom.

Let us note that it is not the "gift of knowledge" nor the "gift of wisdom" but the "word of knowledge"

The Gifts of the Spirit

and the "word of wisdom". It is a light given at an opportune moment in order that we may take the necessary decision or may avoid a danger.

I give the example that we read in the Acts of the Apostles: The Holy Spirit directed Paul clearly that he had to go to Jerusalem. He was "led by the Spirit to do so". There was something internal, a personal direction of God for him. Nevertheless by the gift of the word of knowledge the disciples acting through the Holy Spirit exhorted Paul not to go up to Jerusalem (Acts 21:4) and also further on in verse 10 the Scripture says:

> "And as we tarried there many days, there came down from Judea a certain prophet, named Agabus. And when he was come to us, he took Paul's girdle and bound his own hands and feet and said Thus says the Holy Spirit so shall the Jews at Jerusalem bind the man that owns this girdle and shall deliver him into the hands of the Gentiles. And when we heard these things, both we, and they of that place, besought him not to go up to Jerusalem. Then Paul answered, why do you weep and break my heart? For I am ready not to be bound only, but also to die at Jerusalem for the name of the Lord Jesus. And when he would not be persuaded, we ceased, saying, the will of the Lord be done" (Acts 21:10–14).

The Gifts of the Spirit

Although through the gift of the word of knowledge, Paul was warned of what awaited him in Jerusalem, the Lord had already told him that he, Paul, should go and he was ready for everything, even death.

If God, through the word of knowledge warns you that something is going to happen, it is not necessarily the will of God that it should happen. The word of knowledge warns us of what may occur, but it is not necessarily an order from God, rather a warning from God. Wisdom consists of knowing what to do about the word of knowledge that God has revealed.

It took me many years to learn this lesson and I hope that this warning may serve as a caution to those who go about looking for "words" without searching for the Face of God and without obeying the Spiritual principles clearly expressed in His word as to the Government of God in His church.

It was by the gift of the word of knowledge that Peter knew that Ananias and Sapphira were sinning and the judgment of God that fell upon them instilled fear into the Church and God was glorified and the Church was purified.

Each gift operates through the Spirit for the benefit of the Church and without this operation we are losing a powerful weapon for the destruction of Satan's hidden works.

On another occasion, as I was entering my church, I saw a woman talking to the pianist. I didn't know her at all, but the Spirit gave me this word "viper". As I had no word of wisdom, I didn't know what to do with this knowledge and in the end she was used by Satan to disseminate false visions and prophecies to deceive the people and destroy a church, ruining seven years of hard work and sacrifice and wounding the sheep.

The image of a viper is of something deadly and hidden. It has its own camouflage and hides in order to later attack its victim. This is the way our enemy works, taking advantage of the naivety and ignorance of the people, in order to harm the work of God. The spirits of deception and intimidation are wreaking havoc in the world and we need the wisdom from above to avoid falling into the trap.

By a word we read of in James 3:15-17, we can see the difference between the wisdom of the flesh or the devil, and the true wisdom:

> "This wisdom descends not from above, but is earthly, sensual, devilish. But the wisdom that is from above is first pure, then peaceable, gentle, and easy to be entreated, full of mercy and good fruits, without partiality and without hypocrisy."

The Gift of Discerning of Spirits

This gift completes the three gifts of revelation by which fragments or pieces of the mind of God are revealed to us. Something of what is in the omniscient mind of God can be revealed to us through these three gifts.

The Gifts of the Spirit

This gift of discernment of spirits is a supernatural revelation operating through the Holy Spirit. This gift should not be confused with the natural knowledge of existing spiritual conditions. As the text says, the gift of "discernment of spirits" is not a gift for discerning the faults and shortcomings of others. We all have a natural "gift" of criticizing and finding faults and shortcomings in others. What we need is the grace and love of God in order to find something good in every person and to restrain our tongues. This gift is for discerning the character of the spirit that is working in a particular individual, whether it is of God or of Satan. In these last days, as the manifestation of the Antichrist approaches, we are warned not to believe every spirit.

> "Beloved, believe not every spirit but try the spirits whether they are of God" (1 John 4:1).

Not every miracle or sign is a working of God; therefore we must know that the spirit of the Antichrist is already at work in this world: "Even him, whose coming is after the working of Satan with all power and signs and lying wonders." (2 Thessalonians 2:9).

The gift of the discernment of spirits will reveal "deceiving spirits and doctrines of demons" (1Timothy 4:1). In these days when Spiritism is growing and winning souls for this accursed teaching, this gift is of great importance in order to be able to discern these false spirits. Even apart from this gift however, we have certain

The Gifts of the Spirit

unquestionable ways by which we can discern what kinds of spirits they are. Christ said: "You shall know them by their fruits. Do men gather grapes of thorns, or figs of thistles? Even so every good tree brings forth good fruit; but a corrupt tree brings forth evil fruit. A good tree can not bring forth evil fruit, neither can a corrupt tree bring forth good fruit" (Matthew 7:16-18).

We can summarize this entire subject by saying that if there is the true Spirit of God, there is also a false or lying spirit (compare John 16:13 with John 8:44). If we can see the Holy Spirit do miracles and wonders, there will be the imitation of Satan with lying activities. If there are ministers full of the Spirit of God preaching the truth, there will be deceiving ministers preaching false and demonic doctrines (see 1Timothy 4:1). We must say here that although the doctrine is true there remains the possibility that the messenger may be a deceiver although what he says is true. Note the case of the fortune-telling girl who revealed truth about Paul with crooked motives to try to ruin the testimony of the servant of God. For many days Paul continued preaching while the spirit of fortune telling followed him.

Besides, the Bible says as well: "hereby know you the spirit of God: Every spirit that confesses that Jesus Christ is come in the flesh is of God." (1 John 4:2). We hear more and more of false doctrines denying the supernatural birth of Christ by the Virgin Mary; of a gospel without power and salvation without the blood of Christ. Reject all

The Gifts of the Spirit

these teachings of the devil because" ... without shedding of blood is no remission" (Hebrews 9:22). To the extent that miracles and signs are done you can know they are of God because they are done in the name of Jesus Christ and done to glorify God.

When an impostor tries to cast out demons in the name of Christ the same will happen to him as to the sons of Sceva who were overpowered by the foul spirit and fled naked and injured.

> "Then certain of the vagabond Jews, exorcists, took upon them to call over them which had evil spirits the name of the Lord Jesus, saying, We adjure you by Jesus whom Paul preaches. And there were seven sons of one Sceva, a Jew, and chief of the priests, which did so. And the evil spirit answered and said, Jesus I know and Paul I know, but who are you? And the man in whom the evil spirit was leaped on them, and overcame them, so that they fled out of that house naked and wounded" (Acts 19:13-16).

In the subject of discerning of spirits, we should note that there are three spirits which act and speak through a person. The Spirit of God, the spirit of Satan or the spirit of man, that is, the human spirit. In order to fight the increasing influence in the world that is bringing deception and false teachings, we need the supernatural power of God and the supernatural gifts of the Spirit.

The Gifts of the Spirit

"For we wrestle not against flesh and blood, but against principalities, against powers, against the rulers of the darkness of this world, against spiritual wickedness in high places" (Ephesians 6:12).

The devil has come down with great rage, but we are not defenceless against him. Jesus said: "Behold, I give to you power to tread on serpents and scorpions and over all the power of the enemy: and nothing shall by any means hurt you" (Luke 10:19).

It has been my personal experience that without the operation of the discerning of spirits I have not had the power, or the faith, to cast out demons. When this gift was operating, we have had the victory on practically every occasion. I don't say this by way of a rule, but as my personal experience. This does not necessarily have to be your experience. The Holy Spirit in us sets us free from all oppression by the exercise of faith; and in the name of Jesus Christ every demon and every satanic spirit has to leave.

The Lord himself said:" But if I with the finger of God cast out devils, no doubt the kingdom of God is come upon you" (Luke 11:20).

This gift manifests itself also for the discernment of spirits of error working in the sons of Satan, transformed as ministers of light and righteousness. (See 2 Corinthians 11:14-15). Besides, this gift is useful for discerning prophecies

The Gifts of the Spirit

and supernatural expressions. It is also used to know what satanic spirit is working in the possessed person; for example, it can be a spirit of witchcraft, a deaf and dumb spirit, an unclean spirit, or a spirit of lust, of fear etc...

We can summarise this entire subject by saying that if there is the true Spirit of God, there is also a false or lying spirit. (compare John 16:13 with John 8:44) If we can see the manifestation of the Holy Spirit in performing miracles and wonders, there will be the imitation of Satan with lying wonders. If there are ministers full of the Spirit of God, preaching the truth, there will be deceiving ministers preaching false doctrines of demons (see 1Timothy 4:1).

We must say here that although the doctrine is true there remains the possibility that the messenger may be a deceiver although what he says is true. Note the case of the fortune-telling girl who revealed truth about Paul with crooked motives to try to ruin the testimony of the servant of God. For many days Paul continued preaching while the spirit of fortune telling followed him.

> "The same followed Paul and us, and cried saying: these men are the servants of the most high God, which show to us the way of salvation. And this did she many days But Paul, being grieved, turned, and said to the spirit, I command you in the name of Jesus Christ to come out of her. And he came out the same

The Gifts of the Spirit

hour" (Acts 16: 17-18).

When the Spirit of God came upon Paul, the gift operated in him. The enemy often sends messengers to befriend the sons of God and thus try to ruin them, or lead them astray into error.

If there is the gift of the word of knowledge and Wisdom revealing the mind of God to His children, there will also be the voice of Satan revealing his ideas to the spiritists.

If we are filled with the Spirit and grounded in the Word of God, seeking only the glory of God, then we shall have no difficulty in discerning the spirits. Let us trust in our good Shepherd and He will guide us along the paths of righteousness into all truth.

"For as many are led by the Spirit of God, they are the sons of God" (Romans 8:14).

The Gifts of Healings

The gifts of healings operate in the believer by a special anointing of the Spirit for the healing of the sick person. It is completely supernatural and should in no way be confused with the natural gifts or the intelligence given to medical doctors. The gifts of healings are operated by the Holy Spirit in the believer who is full of faith and power.

"But the manifestation of the Spirit is given to every man to profit withal" (1 Corinthians 12:7).

The Gifts of the Spirit

In the sense that God is the One who created and who puts in order the laws of nature, we can conclude by saying that it is God who heals through medical science, doctors, medicine etc.

In the strict meaning of the word, medical science operates through the natural laws and not through the laws of the Spirit. God's plan for the Church concerning healing the sick is the prayer of faith and the gifts of healings.

The path of the world is that of medical science, but the purpose of the Spirit is through faith and in the supernatural power of God. Certainly we must give credit to the medical profession and to medical science for all the good they have achieved for humanity by their lives dedicated to trying to cure or relieve diseases. In the same way we can be grateful to farmers who cultivate the fruits, vegetables etc... and for the livestock they raise for our use.

Nonetheless a pure atheist can be a good agriculturist or doctor. Although Luke was a doctor, when Christ sent him to "heal the sick and cast out demons", he did this work in the power of the Holy Spirit, and not by his natural intelligence nor by psychiatry.

The gifts of healings are plural as is understood by the word "gifts". They are not restricted to one type of operation, but there are many ways through which they work. They are always operated by the Holy Spirit in the believer and not by the will of

The Gifts of the Spirit

man. If God has given the gifts of healings to the Church, we can conclude that it is His will to continue healing the sick in the present day.

The presence of faith is always necessary for the exercise of these gifts just as it is for the other spiritual gifts. Faith is always required in the one who ministers and also should be in the person receiving. In the event of the sick person being so ill that he cannot exercise his faith, then the faith of the one ministering will be sufficient. There have been cases where the sick person, being untaught and unbelieving, has been healed by the faith of the minister, but this should not be considered the rule, but rather the exception. When there is much faith present in the meeting, it is much easier for the gifts of healings to operate. Despite the sick having little faith, God can work miracles of healing through the faith of the minister and that of the other believers. There are special services where these gifts are manifested more than in others, in accordance with the intention of the Spirit and the need present. These gifts are very useful in evangelism. Nothing draws attention to Christ like the miracles and wonders that accompany the ministry of the Evangelist with the gifts of healings.

The ministry of Christ was well known for His works of healing operated among the sick.

> "And Jesus went about all the cities and villages, teaching in their synagogues, and preaching the gospel of the kingdom, and healing every sickness and every

disease among the people" (Matthew 9:35).

When John the Baptist sent his disciples to ask Christ about who He really was, the Lord proclaimed He was the Messiah through the healing works He was doing. Jesus said: "The blind receive their sight, and the lame walk, the lepers are cleansed, and the deaf hear, the dead are raised up" (Matthew 11:5).

Before the disciples received the baptism in the Holy Spirit, Christ conferred on them a special anointing "... He gave them power against unclean spirits to cast them out, and to heal all manner of sickness and all manner all disease" (Matthew 10:1).

The gifts of healings operated strongly in Peter for we read that: "Insomuch that they brought forth the sick into the streets and laid them on beds and couches, that at the least the shadow of Peter passing by might overshadow some of them ... and they were healed everyone" (Acts 5:15-16). By the gifts of healings, the healing power of Christ was manifested in His servants wiping out diseases and casting out every spirit of sickness.

The gifts of healings operated in Philip the Evangelist, for the scripture says: "And the people with one accord gave heed to those things which Philip spoke, hearing and seeing the miracles which he did" (Acts 8:6).

The Gifts of the Spirit

The gifts of healings operated in Paul also. "And God wrought special miracles by the hands of Paul.

So that from his body were brought to the sick handkerchiefs or aprons, and the diseases departed from them and the evil spirits went out of them" (Acts 19:11-12).

We can note the various kinds of the gifts of healings which operated through the laying on of hands, through Peter's shadow, and still by the handkerchiefs and aprons that had touched the body of Paul.

I think we must clarify that God not only heals through the gifts of healings, but also through the believer's faith in the substitutionary work of Christ.

> "And who (Christ) Himself bore our sins in His own body on the tree... by whose stripes you were healed" (1 Peter 2:24).

With the working of the gifts of healings, and the working of miracles and faith, it is much easier for the sick person to be set free, even if his faith is weak and his condition so serious that he cannot exercise it. We know that "everything is possible to him who believes"; however, God has put gifts of healing in the Church fully aware of our weakness and our lack of faith.

The Gifts of the Spirit

The healing that is received through this gift can be immediate or gradual, according to the circumstances. The lepers that were healed by Christ "were cleansed as they went" in obedience to the Word of the Lord (see Luke 17:12-14).

The blind man whose eyes Jesus anointed with clay, "came back seeing" after he had washed in the pool of Siloam. (see John 9:1-7). Others were healed immediately as in the case of Aeneas when Peter said to him: "Aeneas, Jesus Christ maketh thee whole: arise, and make thy bed." And he arose immediately" (Acts 9:34).

Let us note the effect that the operation of these gifts had on the people. In the case of the Aeneas' healing, the Bible declares that: "So all who dwelt at Lydda and Sharon saw him and turned to the Lord (Acts 9:35) In the same chapter of Acts we have the miracle of Dorcas' resurrection, where also through this miracle "many believed in the Lord" (Acts 9:36–43). In Philipp's ministry, healings which confirmed his preaching, also crowds in Samaria were converted and "they were baptized men and women" (see Acts 8:12). By the healings and miracles carried out in the Name of Jesus Christ, God is glorified and many were convinced of the truth of the Gospel. The same Gospel, which has the power to work the miracle of transforming lives and cleansing them of all sin, is also powerful to heal sick bodies. The healing of the body shows the infinite love of God in Christ Jesus. "Surely, He (Christ) has born our griefs, and carried our sorrows" (Isaiah 53:4).

The Gifts of the Spirit

Christ is still "Jehovah your Healer" working by means of His servants, the works of healing and proving to the world that "Jesus Christ is the same yesterday and today and forever" (Hebrews 13:8).

The Lord worked through His disciples confirming the Word with signs following and He is the same who works with His disciples today. The gifts of healings are for today and must be operating in the Body of Christ.

The Gift of Working of Miracles

The workings of miracles are done supernaturally in the natural plane, transcending the laws of nature. Miracles are God's intervention in human affairs. Frequently the gifts of healings and the working of miracles operate together in the ministry of the Evangelist. The early church was expectant in faith that healings and miracles would follow the preaching of the Word of God. When they were persecuted by the priests and elders, the disciples, fervent and unanimous in their prayer, entreated God "... by stretching forth your hand to heal; and that signs and wonders may be done by the name of your Holy Child Jesus" (Acts 4:30). They expected that the Lord would work with them confirming the Word with healing and miracles. The workings of miracles can operate physical healings; also it can operate on inanimate objects and in nature. In the Old Testament we have countless references to miracles done by God through His servants who were full of faith.

"Who through faith subdued kingdoms,

The Gifts of the Spirit

wrought righteousness, obtained promises, stopped the mouth of lions. Quenched the violence of fire, escaped the edge of the sword, out of weakness were made strong, waxed valiant in fight, turned to flight the armies of the aliens. Women received their dead raised to life again, and others were tortured not accepting deliverance that they might obtain a better resurrection" (Hebrews 11:33–35).

It would be impossible to cover here all the workings of miracles mentioned in the Bible, but briefly I want to give some examples to explain the operation of this gift and its part in the plan of God. Our God is a "miraculous God" and for Him there is no miracle. That which is contrary to natural laws we call miracles, but for God a miracle is something ordinary or natural.

Let us note the working of miracles in the area of the inanimate, in the ministry of Elisha. The sons of the prophets were building their "Bible College" and "It happened that as one of them was felling a beam the iron head of the axe fell into the water... so the man of God asked: Where did it fall? And when he was shown the place, he cut down a stick and threw it in there; and he made the iron float" (2 King 6:5-6). By the working of miracles, Elisha changed the law of Nature, causing the iron to come to the surface of the water.

The Gifts of the Spirit

In the ministry of his predecessor, Elijah, we see a miracle working in the area of Nature. "Then Elijah took his mantle and wrapped it together and smote the waters, and they were divided here and there so that the two went over on dry ground" (2 Kings 2:8).

God worked seven miracles in the life of Elijah, and fourteen through Elisha, who received a double portion of His Spirit (see 2 Kings 2:9). Only thirteen miracles were operated during his lifetime and the last one was after his death. "And it came to pass as they were burying a man, that, behold, they spied a band of men, and they cast the man into the sepulchre of Elisha, and when the man was let down and touched the bones of Elisha, he revived and stood upon his feet" (2 Kings 13:21).

We have many examples of miracles in the area of Nature in Christ's ministry. Peter had worked all the night fishing, but had caught nothing. On the instructions of Christ, he cast his net and they were unable to pull it out on account of the great quantity of fish (see John 21:3,5,6). It was the working of a miracle that drew the fish to that place so that they got in the net, thereby showing the glory of God and paying the disciples generously for lending their boat to Christ. One day the disciples were sailing over a lake and Christ was sleeping in the boat; while they were sailing a wind storm overtook them giving them great fear of its danger. "And they came to Him and awoke Him, saying, Master, Master, we are perishing! Then He arose and rebuked the wind and the raging of the water.

The Gifts of the Spirit

And they ceased, and there was a calm" (Luke 8:24).

Through the use of this gift, Christ reprimanded the wind and showed the power of God over Nature and the fury of the sea.

On another occasion Jesus changed the natural laws, by walking upon the sea (see Matthew 14:25). A miracle in the physical area that happened twice was the miracle of the loaves, when Jesus broke them and fed them to the multitudes (Matthew 14:13-21 and 15:32-39), confirming thus His eternal covenant as "Jehovah Jireh" which translated is "Jehovah will provide". In the commencement of His ministry, Christ supplied what was necessary in the wedding feast of Cana in Galilee where He changed six jars of water into wine. "This beginning of miracles did Jesus in Cana of Galilee and manifested forth His glory; and His disciples believed on Him" (John 2:11).

In the area of healing, the Lord performed a miracle in raising Lazarus from the dead; who had been dead already four days (see John 11:39,43,44). A miracle was worked in raising from the dead the widow's son (see Luke 7:12,14,15), and the ruler of the synagogue, Jairus' daughter, (see Luke 8:41-42) and many other instances.

Christ did these miracles through the Gift of the Working of Miracles and not through His divinity. He gave up His glory, took upon himself the form of a man, and was tempted in everything according to

The Gifts of the Spirit

our likeness, but without sin (see Hebrews 4:15). Although He was the Son of God, He did not use His divinity, "And having been perfected, He became the author of eternal salvation to all who obey Him" (Hebrews 5:9).

"Therefore, in all things He had to be made like His brethren, that He might be a merciful and faithful High Priest in things pertaining to God, to make propitiation for the sins of the people" (Hebrews 2:17). The Lord promised: "Verily, verily, I say to you, He that believes on me, the works that I do, shall he do also, and greater works than these shall he do because I go to my Father" (John 14:12).

With the outpouring of the Holy Spirit, this gift like the others, has been given to the Church as shown in the book of the Acts of the Apostles; and although a miracle is a supernatural act, divinely inspired, the Lord has desired to give the manifestation of this power to His children. Christ did not reserve this gift solely for His own use, but for the Church today. Jesus said: "Whosoever shall say to this mountain, be removed and be cast into the sea and shall not doubt in his heart, but shall believe that these things which he said shall come to pass, he shall have whatever he says" (Mark 11:23). Through the operation of this gift, the necessary faith is active in working miracles for the glory of God.

Saint Paul found himself in need of this gift when "he shook off the beast into the fire and suffered no harm" (Acts 28:5). Saint Peter was operating in this gift when he raised Tabitha from the dead (see Acts

The Gifts of the Spirit

9:40). By the Lord's command to heal the sick and raise the dead (see Matthew 10:8). Peter was able to have the necessary faith to exercise this gift.

We likewise can trust that God will be present confirming His Word with wonders and miracles to supply any need.

When there was the necessity that Philip should go quickly to Azotus, "the Spirit of the Lord caught Philip away ...and was found at Azotus" (see Acts 8:39,40). I don't say that in this case it was the working of the gift, for there is no evidence to show that Philip exercised his faith, but rather it was the manifestation of the sovereign will of God. When God wished to take Paul and Silas out of the prison, the Lord caused an earthquake: "Suddenly there was a great earthquake, so that the foundations of the prison were shaken; and immediately all the doors were opened and everyone's chains were loosed" (Acts 16:26). By their actions of praise and faith, they created the atmosphere for a miracle that resulted in their being released and in the conversion of the prison warden and his family. The working of this gift is with the co-operation of the will of the person, when he/she is inspired by God in believing for a miracle. God can work miracles even without the co-operation of man, but in this instance it is not the operation of the gift, rather the sovereign will of God.

We can conclude by saying that God is powerful to work miracles when His servants, full of faith, seek

The Gifts of the Spirit

to fulfil his commands. It is clear that if we do not expect a miracle nor believe that God can do it, then certainly, we shall not receive it. If you need a miracle in your life, only believe, and you will see the glory of God!

> "Therefore I say to you, whatsoever things you desire when you pray, believe that you have already received them and you shall have them" (Marc 11:24).

The manifestation of this gift, like the others always glorifies and exalts Christ, and very often causes the conversion of crowds. In Samaria multitudes believed and were baptised, seeing the miracles and great wonders that were being done. Through the resurrection of Lazarus from the dead, many of the Jews believed because of him. When Tabitha was raised from the dead, this became widely known throughout Joppa, and many believed in the Lord. Not everyone has the "faculty to work miracles", but it is for us to desire and be zealous of the spiritual gifts. These gifts combined with the love of God, are God's divine purpose for these perilous times.

The Gift of Faith

The gift of faith is the supernatural imparting of faith by the Holy Spirit. This is not the natural faith that everyone possesses according to his ability, nor a fruit of the Spirit in the believer. This gift is the faith of God given in the moment of necessity to work miracles, wonders and healings. The person who has this gift cannot operate it by his own will,

The Gifts of the Spirit

but as in the case of all the gifts, it is operated according to the will of the Holy Spirit.

With the imparting of the gift of faith, the answer to his prayer is assured to the believer. It is different in its working from the "prayer of faith", although both are inspired by the Holy Spirit. The prayer of faith is the prayer of the Spirit where our faith is inspired and increased. When the gift of faith is working, on the whole, the results are brought about immediately. The prayer of faith is also prayed in the Spirit and the answer is assured in the heart of the person although he may have to wait, if necessary, several years to see its fulfilment.

A certain man lying sick in bed was burdened in prayer for a number of missionary fields. In his diary after having sensed the victory in prayer, wrote saying: "Today I have prayed, what I sense is the prayer of faith for a particular place". After some time this brother died and his wife showed his diary to a minister. They saw that God had sent revival in all the places, almost in the given order, and through the prayer of faith this servant of God prevailed.

In the case of the prayer of faith, our faith is inspired and increased by the Holy Spirit praying in us, giving us the confidence that God has heard our prayer and that He shall answer it. The gift of faith is the participation of the faith of God, given to the believer in an instant to work according to the will of God. We can conclude by saying that

The Gifts of the Spirit

this gift is the most important of the three gifts of power, giving the faculty to work miracles, healings, wonders etc. This gift works in any area of human need and is unlimited in its potential.

In the case of the lame man at the temple's gate called "Beautiful", we can see this gift working in combination with the gift of healing for the immediate recovery of the lame man. This man, lame since birth, received complete healing even without any evidence of his personal faith. It was the gift, working in Peter and John which gave these servants the confidence to command him: "Rise and walk" (Acts 3:6). Peter confirmed that it was not by their virtue or holiness that the man was healed, but by the faith of Christ.

> "And His name, through faith in His name, has made this man strong, whom you see and know. Yes, the faith which comes through Him has given him this perfect soundness in the presence of you all" (Acts 3:16).

It is very probable that Peter and John would have passed by several times where this man was, on their way to the temple at the hour of prayer. Because it is written that the lame man was "whom they laid daily at the gate of the temple" (Acts 3:2) God in His omniscience chose that day for performing this "miracle of healing" and thus coordinated all the activities of His servants for His glory.

The Gifts of the Spirit

Besides being a marvellous work, this gift is sometimes bestowed in times of disaster and anguish, giving the believer an assurance and a peace that appears he could not have in any other way. By the working of faith Christ was able to say to Mary: "Your brother will rise" (see John 11:23). By faith Paul was able to affirm to the terrified sailors that: "For there shall not fall a hair of any of you" (Acts 27:34). Through the operation of faith the three Hebrew youngsters were able to say: "Our God whom we serve is able to deliver us from the burning fiery furnace, and he will deliver us from your hand, O king" (Daniel 3:17).

Our faith in God is necessary "... and without faith it is impossible to please Him" (see Hebrews 11:6). Nevertheless, there will be times when the impartation of this supernatural faith is necessary in our lives.

We can conclude this subject with the words of Paul, who said: "Though I have all faith so that I could remove mountains but have not love, I am nothing" (1 Corinthians 13:2). The gifts must have their roots in love. Love is the greatest of God's attribute that we receive from Him. Faith and love are eternal, because God is eternal.

> "And now abides faith, hope, and love, these three, but the greatest of these is love" (1Corinthians 13:13).

True faith works in us by the love of God. Faith and love are two operations of the Spirit of God. The

The Gifts of the Spirit

Holy Spirit has nine manifestations in the nine gifts of the Spirit.

There are seven operations of the Spirit which show His character and His attributes. "I looked and saw in the midst of the throne a Lamb standing as it had been slain... that had seven eyes which are the seven Spirits of God sent into all the earth" (Revelation 5:6).

These seven attributes are:

- The "Spirit of holiness" (see Romans 1:4);
- The "Spirit of grace and supplication" (see Zacharias 12:10);
- The "Spirit of wisdom" (see Isaiah 11:2 and Ephesians 1:17);
- The "Spirit of counsel and of power" (see Isaiah 11:2);
- The "Spirit of knowledge and of fear of the Lord" (see Isaiah 11:2);
- The "Spirit of love" (see 2 Timothy 1:17) and
- The "Spirit of judgement and burning or consuming fire" (see Isaiah 4:4).

The Holy Spirit is one, but He manifests Himself in different ways in accord with His omniscience. As the light is visible in the rainbow in seven colours, so the Holy Spirit has seven characteristics which are revealed to us on different occasions according to what He wishes. Sometimes He manifests His love and sometimes His anger and wrath, just as the circumstances warrant. A father sometimes kisses and hugs his children, and other times he has to chastise them.

God does not change, but his dealings with people vary according to the conditions He finds.

God works in us through His Spirit, instilling His character in us, and manifesting Himself through the nine characteristics of the Spirit. All these gifts have to be grounded and rooted in the "more excellent way", that is, in love.

Amen.

CHAPTER 9
LOVE

"Though I speak with the tongues of men and of angels, and have not love, I am become as sounding brass, or a tinkling cymbal. And though I have the gift of prophecy, and understand all mysteries, and all knowledge; And though I have all faith, so that I could remove mountains, and have not love, I am nothing. And though I bestow all my goods to feed the poor, and though I give my body to be burned, and have not love, it profits me nothing" (1 Corinthians 13:1-3).

The love of God takes away all fear

Love is of God, because God is love (see 1 John 4:7,8). Spiritual love is the devotion which is deliberate and inspired by God's love in us and for us. Just as the rays of the sun dispel darkness and bring warmth and health, so the love of God shines on the world. If we open the windows of our faculties to God's love, that love will come in, freeing us from fear, sadness and evil. Love is the most sublime and divine virtue that we receive from the heart of God. And he who walks in and directs his entire life by that love will walk in the light of God. "He that loves his brother abides in the light, and there is no occasion of stumbling in him" (1 John 2:10).

Love

Love is the greatest force in maintaining the unity of the church. This Love is the most excellent and most fragrant characteristic of Christ. Christ understands better than anyone else the urges of love and is always ready to justify and forgive those who love. An example of reciprocal love is in the story of the adulterous woman, who once she has been cleansed and set free shows her love for Jesus.

> "And, behold, a woman in the city, which was a sinner, when she knew that Jesus sat at meat in the Pharisee's house, brought an alabaster box of ointment. And stood at his feet behind him weeping, and began to wash his feet with tears, and did wipe them with the hairs of her head, and kissed his feet, and anointed them with the ointment" (Luke 7:37,38).

The Lord rebuked the Pharisee for his criticism of the woman declaring that by her great love she received great blessing. "Wherefore I say to you, her sins, which are many, are forgiven; for she loved much: but to whom little is forgiven, the same loves little" (Luke 7:47).

Love is eternal and never ceases to exist because it emanates from the "Alpha and the Omega", God. Love is the inspiration of progress and perfection in all mankind. Love is the perfection of all the gifts and grace to which we shall attain. This love demands sacrifice and self-denial more than anything else would.

Love

"For God so loved the world, that he gave His only begotten Son, that whosoever believes in Him should not perish, but have everlasting life" (John 3:16).

God showed us perfect love by giving us His Son to save us from eternal death

The world is being impoverished rapidly in the matter of love. The law courts full of divorce cases bear silent testimony to the spoils of sin with its attack on love, the most precious gift that God has given. God has given to everyone the ability to love. This human love, though great and sublime has its limits. Human love is imperfect and is frequently rooted in selfishness. In most cases human love is to get and obtain. Only God showed us perfect love by giving His only begotten Son in order to save us from eternal death.

"Yet it pleased the Lord to bruise him; He has put him to grief: when you have made his soul an offering for sin, he shall see his seed, he shall prolong his days, and the pleasure of the Lord shall prosper in his hand" (Isaiah 53:10).

If you can fathom the depth of this verse, you will be able to understand the heart of God. Christ showed this perfect love when He gave up His life on the cruel cross for us while we were yet sinners. From His bloodstained lips we can hear the voice of love triumphant over all the evils, cruelty and selfishness in the world. "Then said Jesus: Father forgive them; for they know not what they do" (Luke 23:34).

This is the love of God, in Greek "Agape", the love which never ceases.

> "Love suffers long and is kind; love envies not; love vaunts not itself, is not puffed up. Does not behave itself unseemly, seeks not her own, is not easily provoked, thinks no evil; Rejoices not in iniquity, but rejoices in the truth; bears all things, believes all things, hopes all things, endures all things. Love never fails" (1 Corinthians 13:4-8).

Though we were to write volumes, we would not be able to add anything to these words which came forth from the heart of God. This is the love of God which must shine in our hearts. Mankind cannot reach this goal. The world is impoverished without this love. It is the salt of life. The ointment that heals, the power that does not know the word impossible, the virtue that does not accept the word sacrifice. Love covers a multitude of sins, does not consider injustice as an alternative, and bears all things.

Above all, we must seek love

Selfishness is the biggest enemy of love. For love does not puff itself up, nor does it seek its own. You must desire the spiritual gifts, but above all things, we must seek love above everything else (see 1 Corinthians 14:1). The music of the love of

Love

God is what is heard in the heavens, the perfection of paradise. The kingdom of God is a kingdom of love and every citizen possesses it.

When Saint Paul refers to love as the more excellent way, he did not mean, that love would nullify the gifts. If this was the meaning it would be superfluous to continue in 1 Corinthians 14:1. "Follow after love, and desire spiritual gifts". The apostle was simply stating that instead of making the obtaining of the gifts one's main aim, the highest and best path is to achieve love and the gifts would still have their rightful place.

The gifts are partial and temporal, until perfection has come, which we shall receive when we see Jesus face to face. "For now we see through a glass, darkly; but then face to face: now I know in part; but then shall I know even as also I am known" (1 Corinthians 13:12). When the veil of the physical body and human condition is removed; then it shall be when we are in the presence of the King of Glory and we shall know as we are known.

Love purifies and matures the gifts of the Spirit in us. Love is eternal; it will ensure that the fruit harvested by the gifts will last. Persevere with love, make it the most sublime longing in the perfecting of your spiritual life. In looking at the love revealed in Christ we can know at what distance we still are from the goal. Even in the most talented and gifted servants of God, we can observe the lack of this divine virtue. Love produces the humility which is characteristic of the humble Master. The love of

God made manifest in us is the fulfillment of the law.

> "Jesus said to him: You shall love the Lord your God with all your heart, and with all your soul, and with all your mind. This is the first and greatest commandment. And the second is like it, you shall love your neighbour as yourself. On these two commandments hang all the law and the prophets" (Matthew 22:37-40).

Love one another

To love one another is the commandment that Christ has given us: "A new commandment I give to you, that you love one another; as I have loved you, that you also love one another" (John 13:34). Not only to love one another, but rather to love as He has loved us.

> "Fulfil my joy, that you be likeminded, having the same love, being of one accord, of one mind" (Philippians 2:2).

"But I say to you, love your enemies, bless them that curse you, do good to them that hate you, and pray for them which despitefully use you and persecute you" (Matthew 5:44). The secret of attaining this love is to submit ourselves to the power of the love of God. "Be therefore followers of God, as dear children and walk in love" (Ephesians 5:1). In our conduct towards our Christian brothers and the world let God's love be our guide in everything. God's love in us can overcome all the works and affections of the old man. Love is more powerful than selfishness which it overcomes as light shines through darkness.

> "Many waters cannot quench love, nor can the floods drown it. If a man would give for love all the wealth of his house, it would be utterly despised" (Song of Solomon 8:7).

Christ's love overcame the cruel temptation of Satan, overcame the shame of the cross, and overcame the cup of torture in the garden of Gethsemane. "And now abides faith, hope, love, these three; but the greatest of these is love" (1 Corinthians 13:13).

God's purpose for His church, His body here on earth is described in Ephesians 3:17-19:

> "That Christ may dwell in your hearts through faith; that you, being rooted and grounded in love, may be able to comprehend with all the saints what is the width and length and depth and height; to know the love of Christ which passes knowledge; that you may be filled with all the fullness of God".

In order to be to be filled with the fullness of God, it is necessary to know the love of God, and to be sure that He loves us and cares for us. Saint Peter understood this for he wrote: "Casting all your care upon Him; for He cares for you." (1 Peter 5:7).

Love

These words inspire us to continue praying and putting our trust in God despite adverse circumstances and when we cannot understand what is happening.

Amen.

CHAPTER 10

DIVINE HEALING

"Surely He has borne our griefs and carried our sorrows; Yet we esteemed Him stricken, smitten by God, and afflicted. But He was wounded for our transgressions; He was bruised for our iniquities; The chastisement for our peace was upon Him, and by His stripes we are healed" (Isaiah 53:4,5).

Is it God's will that we should be healed?

The doctrine of Divine Healing is so important that I have decided to devote a whole chapter to deal briefly with this subject. There is so much ignorance about God's will concerning healing, that I am going to clarify conclusively God's will as it is revealed in His Word. It is impossible to pray in faith without knowing God's Will. We can know the will of God by the Holy Bible, by the Holy Spirit, and at times by the very circumstances. As to divine healing it is unnecessary to pray "if it is your will, Lord", because God has clearly revealed His will in this matter.

In addition to the evidence of Scripture, the life and ministry of Christ is sufficient in as far as He has come to do and reveal God's will to us. In all His works and words He revealed God's will to the world.

Divine Healing

Peter speaks of Christ's ministry as follows:

> "How God anointed Jesus of Nazareth with the Holy Spirit and with power: who went about doing good, and healing all that were oppressed of the devil; for God was with him" (Acts 10:38).

Here sickness is classified as "the oppression of the devil" and not from God. If sickness had been sent by God, then Christ would have healed against God's will because He healed all.

If sickness was sent by God, then hospitals would be houses of rebellion rather than houses of mercy. If sickness was sent by God, then doctors and nurses would be rebels because they strive to heal or relieve suffering. Sickness has come because of sin, as a part of the curse of the law!

Through Christ's sacrifice we can be set free of the curse of the law. This includes salvation for the soul and healing for the body.

> "Christ has redeemed us from the curse of the law, having become a curse for us" (Galatians 3:13).

God has promised: "And the Lord will take away from you all sickness" (Deuteronomy 7:15).
Through these redemptive Names, the Lord reveals His will to us.

Divine Healing

Names	Scriptural quotation
Jehovah-Shamma. Ezekiel 48:35.	The Lord is there.
Jehovah-Shalom. Judges 6:24.	The Lord is peace.
Jehovah-Ra-ha. Psalm 23:1.	The lord is my shepherd.
Jehovah-Jireh. Genesis 22:14.	The Lord will provide.
Jehovah-Nissi. Exodus 17:15.	The Lord is my banner.
Jehovah-Tsidkenu. Jeremiah 23:6.	The Lord, our righteousness.
Jehovah-Rapha. Exodus 15:26.	I, the Lord am your healer.

If God revealed Himself in the law as the Healer of Israel, healing three million people, how much more shall we be healed in these times, in the dispensation of Grace, by means of the work of Jesus Christ. Christ has been made a curse for us and on the cross. He took away our sins and our sicknesses.

> "Who his own self bare our sins in his own body on the tree, that we, being dead to sins, should live to righteousness by whose stripes you were healed" (1 Peter 2:24).

Divine Healing

Jesus won the victory for us, over sin, death and sickness

The work of Christ is as complete as our redemption. When He said: "It is finished", He won for us the victory over sin, death and sickness. The words "you were healed" reveal that, as far as God is concerned, we are already healed. Healing and health belong to us because we have been bought with the blood of Christ. You don't have to suffer the afflictions of any disease nor bear what Christ bore for you. We have to bear our cross in serving and following Christ, but this cross is not a cross of sickness. When Paul spoke of his thorn in the flesh, in no way did it refer to sickness as many people wrongly think. He clearly stated that it was a messenger of Satan and not a disease. It was simply a demon that brought upon him "abuses, hardship, persecution and anguish... for when I am weak, then I am strong" (2 Corinthians 12:10). Instead of delivering him from these abuses, from this persecution, etc. God gave him His Grace to bear it. Because of this, he could say: "When I am weak, (not sick) then I am strong".

We must be brave and resolutely confess our faith in God's Word.

"For with the heart one believes unto righteousness, and with the mouth confession is made unto salvation", or (health) according to other versions (Romans 10:10).

Divine Healing

Just as we had to believe and confess Christ as Lord to be saved, so must we confess healing.

In Isaiah's text we read: "Surely He has borne our griefs and carried our sorrows; ... and by His stripes we are healed". The prophet by the vision of faith declared the good news of the gospel, centuries before the coming of Christ. The Holy Spirit declared that "we were healed", while speaking of physical sicknesses. Saint Matthew helps us to interpret this scripture when he said: "When the even was come, they brought to him many that were possessed with demons; and he cast out the spirits with his word, and healed all that were sick, that it might be fulfilled which was spoken by the prophet Isaiah, saying: He Himself took our infirmities and bore our sicknesses" (Matthew 8:16,17).

Perhaps you have been like the leper who came to Christ knowing that he could heal him, but uncertain about His will to do so. "And behold, a leper came and worshiped Him, saying, Lord, if You are willing, you can make me clean. Then Jesus put out His hand and touched him, saying, I am willing; be cleansed. Immediately his leprosy was cleansed" (Matthew 8:2,3).

Hear the voice of the Lord when He dismissed the doubts that were tormenting the mind of the leper "I am willing; be cleansed". Jesus Christ continues to be the same now as yesterday; and He wants you also to be clean and whole. Don't remain sitting by the pool of Bethesda suffering (see John 5:2,3).

Divine Healing

Christ has revealed His will for you: "Rise and walk" (see John 5:8). Use your faith in God's Word, show your faith in the Lord; Rise and receive Divine Healing now! "Faith without works is dead" (see James 2:26).

You have now known the will of God as it is revealed in the Holy Bible. Begin now to praise Christ and to bless His Name. "He who forgives all your iniquities, who HEALS all your diseases" (Psalm 103:3). And remember always:

Take God's side,
Never give up, nor lose the faith
And expect a miracle in your life!

Amen.

CHAPTER 11

CASTING OUT DEMONS

"And He said to them, Go into all the world and preach the gospel to every creature. He who believes and is baptized will be saved; but he who does not believe will be condemned. And these signs will follow those who believe: In My name they will cast out demons; they will speak with new tongues; they will take up serpents; and if they drink anything deadly, it will by no means hurt them; they will lay hands on the sick, and they will recover "(Mark 16:15-18).

Many people are suffering ailments and illnesses; the hospitals are always full and try to relieve the ailments of humanity. Innumerable people are suffering mental illnesses, torments, depressions and bondages. Millions have been separated from their families and from their loved ones, and are locked within themselves, behind doors of hospitals for the mentally sick. Jails always have their cells crammed with the captives of evil. Newspapers are always proclaiming through their stories of homicides, rapes and thefts. Billions of dollars are spent yearly trying to stop the rapid growth of juvenile delinquency. Misery, drunkenness, poverty, illnesses, pain, anguish, distress, death, etc... are afflicting more and more in our society. What is the cause? Who is the person mainly

Casting out Demons

responsible for so much pain, disease and misery? The answer is simple and clear: Satan.

Fallen angels from their high position have transformed themselves into evil demons, malignant spirits, whose intention is "to kill, and to steal and to destroy" all the good God has created (compare John 10:10). We are immersed in a spiritual warfare against Satan and his evil hosts. We are sent to destroy his works, to free his prisoners, to cast out demons and to heal those broken by the devil. Satan does not come except to kill, and to steal and to destroy. Because of sin prevailing in the world today, the devil has been able to afflict and move freely among the sons of disobedience. It is sad that even among Gods' children so much disease and oppression prevail due to the ignorance in this matter. The majority of mental patients are the result of demonic activity. Many of the sicknesses are caused by evil spirits sent by Satan. Satanic oppression is the chief motive for anxiety, suicides, addictions, immoralities, homicides and diseases.

It is time for the Church to take the authority given by Christ Jesus and begin to make war against Satan and his work, and that she would arise to challenge and start to cast out demons, heal the sick and set the captives free from the devil. These signs must follow the believers as it was promised in the Word. Every believer has his divine commission and authority to cast out demons and heal the sick. Instead of blaming our failures upon God, we should put it in its rightful place, that is,

Casting out Demons

in our lack of faith. Instead of thinking that God's plan in these last days is different than in the beginning, let's literally believe what is written.

When the disciples failed to cast out a demon, Christ told them that it was because of their lack of faith and that this faith comes through prayer and fasting. It is time for the Church of Christ to know that it is fighting "against principalities, against powers, against the rulers of the darkness of this world, against spiritual wickedness in high places" (Ephesians 6:12). Satan has his work well organized and all his hosts fight furiously against God and good. God needs consecrated people dedicated to the destruction of the works of the devil. Instead of fighting against each other, we must unite against our common enemy!

We have authority against all the work of the devil, as well as for casting out demons and to heal the sick in Jesus' name and through the power of the Holy Spirit. Let us now stand up and act with courage and faith and let us use the glorious name of Jesus Christ for the freedom of the oppressed! We are going to occupy our position in Christ Jesus and use the authority that has been given to us by our risen Captain to fight Satan without rest. Christ is alive to confirm His Word! When He sends us to do His will, He will also give us the strength to fulfil it. As the salt of the earth we have to preserve the world, which is rapidly corrupting itself.

The cause of disease

It is apparent that many diseases are organic in nature and are caused by many factors, however Satan takes advantage of weakness and afflicts our bodies if doors are left open.

By the authority of the Scriptures, we are going to prove that the cause of sicknesses and diseases that afflicts the world is the work of the devil, caused by his spirits of infirmity. The life that produces the disease is malignant, causing pain and death. This power does not come from God but from Satan. Christ came to give us life and life in abundance! He came to destroy the works of Satan.

"For the law of the Spirit of life in Christ Jesus has made me free from the law of sin and death" (Romans 8:2). Saint Peter summarized the ministry of Christ in the following manner:

> "You know how God anointed Jesus of Nazareth with the Holy Spirit and with power, who went about doing good, and healing all that were oppressed of the devil; for God was with him" (Acts 10:38).

Here disease is called "oppression of the devil"; it does not come from God but from Satan whose work is to destroy and to steal health from us. Sickness is not to the Glory of God; God is glorified in health and restoration. Lazarus's death did not praise Christ, but his resurrection did.

Spirits of infirmity

Let's take the story of the woman who walked bent over for eighteen years. Christ clearly said that the infirmity didn't come from God but from the devil. "So ought not this woman, being a daughter of Abraham, whom Satan has bound--think of it--for eighteen years, be loosed from this bond on the Sabbath?" (Luke 13:16).

The Lord did not call this infirmity a blessing sent to try the woman, but rather a bondage from Satan. This had been caused by a spirit of infirmity that attacked her body!

> "And behold, there was a woman who had a spirit of infirmity eighteen years and was bent over and could in no way raise herself up" (Luke 13:11).

These spirits of infirmity that proceed from the devil, attack the body, often in weak areas or which have been infected by a virus or germ. When the healing power of Christ touches the sick person and his faith is exercised, the spirit of infirmity has to leave.

The blind and dumb man

"Then one was brought to Him who was demon-possessed, blind and mute; and He healed him, so that the blind and mute man both spoke and saw" (Mathew 12:22). The blindness of this man was caused by a demon; when Christ healed him, the spirit of blindness left, and he could see. Being dumb was also a work of Satan.

The dumb healed

"As they went out, behold, they brought to Him a man, mute and demon-possessed. And when the demon was cast out, the mute spoke" (Mathew 9:32,33). Here we have another case proving that this disease was caused by a demon.

The deaf and dumb boy.

> "When Jesus saw that the people came running together, He rebuked the unclean spirit, saying to it, Deaf and dumb spirit, I command you, come out of him and enter him no more!" (Mark 9:25).

Here we see that deafness was also caused by an unclean spirit. In my experience in divine healing, almost all cases of deafness that we have encountered have been caused by deaf spirits. God has also healed many cases of epilepsy in my ministry as I have cast out the demons behind it.

As an example I will give the case of a deaf and dumb young man who came to our door asking for alms. He belonged to the society of the deaf and dumb people and brought a notebook to give the corresponding receipt. Apparently he was born this way, and could hear absolutely nothing, nor speak one single word. The sounds that were proceeding from his lips seemed more from an animal rather than from a man.

My wife shared with him the Gospel and the power of God to heal in sign language. He knelt down

Casting out Demons

asking us to pray for him. We prayed with him and by commanding, in the name of Christ, the deaf spirit came out instantly; and he could hear clearly, even the sound of a wrist watch. His dumbness was caused by his deafness. Now, just as a child, he had to learn to speak, since he had never heard sounds. But his ears were completely healed and he could hear clearly.

Unclean spirit

The defilement that is in the world is caused in many cases by the unclean spirits who possess their victims. A man possessed by this spirit was in the Temple, causing disturbance and chaos.

> "Now there was a man in their synagogue with an unclean spirit. And he cried out, saying, "Let us alone! What have we to do with You, Jesus of Nazareth? ... Jesus rebuked him, saying, be quiet, and come out of him!" And when the unclean spirit had convulsed him and cried out with a loud voice, he came out of him" (Mark 1:23-26).

After having seen Jesus, the demon spoke through the lips of the unfortunate possessed person because it was frightened of being cast out. The demons need a body in which to enter in order to express their satanic works. His satanic character was seen and was demonstrated through this man.

In the case of Legion, the demons begged Jesus not to cast them out of that area but rather that he

Casting out Demons

would send them to the great herd of pigs (see Mark 5:12).

The ministry of Christ was full of authority to deliver those who were possessed by demons. The Bible often makes mention of his ministry to cast out demons. "For He healed many, so that as many as had afflictions pressed about Him to touch Him. And the unclean spirits, whenever they saw Him, fell down before Him and cried out, saying, "You are the Son of God" (Mark 3:10-11). The disciples also knew his authority because it was written of them; "And they cast out many demons, and anointed with oil many who were sick, and healed them" (Mark 6:13). They continued with the ministry of deliverance and healing. These occurrences are not merely theory. I have witnessed many of miracles of deliverance for 60 years in many countries.

This power is also for you; it is the power of the Holy Spirit, given to the one that devotes himself to God and knows his authority in Christ. Christ's words are our authority and power until the end of the world.

> "Behold, I give you the authority to trample on serpents and scorpions, and over all the power of the enemy, and nothing shall by any means hurt you" (Luke 10:19).

This commission is also for you, if you can pay the price of prayer and sanctification. "Then He called

Casting out Demons

His twelve disciples together and gave them power and authority over all demons, and to cure diseases" (Luke 9:1).

Multitudes await deliverance and healing. Will you go and take to them the power of God to deliver their lives? God wants to send you and God's power shall be given you if you can believe it. The Spirit of the Lord will come upon you "to proclaim liberty to the captives and to set at liberty those who are oppressed" (see Luke 4:18). You can have authority over all the forces of the devil. You can also heal the sick and cast out demons. Seek the power of God, millions are waiting for it! Christ has sent you to take His Word in all its fullness and power. The signs must follow your ministry, as they did the Apostles of old! The Church needs this ministry more than ever; the world waits for the manifestation of the sons of God. He has called us for three purposes: To be with Him, to preach the gospel and to have power and to heal diseases and to cast out demons (see Mark 3:14-15).

Amen.

Made in the USA
Columbia, SC
28 January 2025